Daily Light

Updated in Today's Language

Daily Light

Samuel Bagster

BARBOUR
PUBLISHING

ISBN 978-1-60260-858-0

Published by Barbour Publishing, Inc., P.O. Box 719, Uhrichsville,
Ohio 44683, www.barbourbooks.com.

*Our mission is to publish and distribute inspirational products offering
exceptional value and biblical encouragement to the masses.*

Printed in the United States of America.

> *The Lord is the One Who goes before you.*
> *He will be with you. He will be faithful*
> *to you and will not leave you alone.*
> *Do not be afraid or troubled.*

If You Yourself do not go with us, do not have us leave this place—O Lord, I know that a man's way is not known by himself. It is not in man to lead his own steps.

The steps of a good man are led by the Lord. And He is happy in his way. When he falls, he will not be thrown down, because the Lord holds his hand.

Yet I am always with You. You hold me by my right hand. You will lead me by telling me what I should do. And after this, You will bring me into shining-greatness— For I know that nothing can keep us from the love of God. Death cannot! Life cannot! Angels cannot! Leaders cannot! Any other power cannot! Hard things now or in the future cannot! The world above or the world below cannot! Any other living thing cannot keep us away from the love of God which is ours through Christ Jesus our Lord.

Deut. 31:8; Exod. 33:15—Jer. 10:23; Ps. 37:23–24; Ps. 73:23–24—Rom. 8:38–39.

Sing for joy to God our strength! Call out for joy to the God of Jacob! Sing a song, beat the timbrel. Play the sweet-sounding harps—He put a new song in my mouth, a song of praise to our God. Many will see and fear and will put their trust in the Lord.

Be strong and have strength of heart! Do not be afraid or lose faith. For the Lord your God is with you anywhere you go—The joy of the Lord is your strength—Paul. . .thanked God and took courage.

You know what time it is. It is time for you to wake up from your sleep. The time when we will be taken up to be with Christ is not as far off as when we first put our trust in Him. Night is almost gone. Day is almost here. We must stop doing the sinful things that are done in the dark. We must put on all the things God gives us to fight with for the day. We must act all the time as if it were day. Keep away from wild parties and do not be drunk. Keep yourself free from sex sins and bad actions. Do not fight or be jealous. Let every part of you belong to the Lord Jesus Christ. Do not allow your weak thoughts to lead you into sinful actions.

Isa. 42:10; Ps. 81:1–2—Ps. 40:3; Josh. 1:9—Neh. 8:10—Acts 28:15—Rom. 13:11–14.

May my prayer be like special perfume before You.
May the lifting up of my hands be like the
evening gift given on the altar in worship.

Make an altar for burning special perfume.... Put this altar in front of the curtain that is by the box of the Law, in front of the mercy-seat that is over the box of the Law. There I will meet with you. Aaron will burn special perfume on it every morning.... And when Aaron takes care of the lamps in the evening, he will burn special perfume. There will be a burning of special perfume before the Lord for all your people for all time.

Jesus is able, now and forever, to save from the punishment of sin all who come to God through Him because <u>He lives forever to pray for them</u>—Smoke from burning the special perfume and the prayers of those who belong to God went up before God out of the angel's hand.

You are to be as living stones in the building God is making also. You are His religious leaders giving yourselves to God through Jesus Christ. This kind of gift pleases God.

Never stop praying.

Ps. 141:2; Exod. 30:1, 6–8; Heb. 7:25—Rev. 8:4; 1 Pet. 2:5; 1 Thess. 5:17.

He found [Jacob] in a desert land, in the empty waste of a desert. He came around him and cared for him. He kept him as He would His own eye. Like an eagle that shakes its nest, that flies over its young, He spread His wings and caught them. He carried them on His wings. The Lord alone led him—Even when you are old I will be the same. And even when your hair turns white, I will help you. I will take care of what I have made. I will carry you, and will save you.

He makes me strong again. He leads me in the way of living right with Himself which brings honor to His name. Yes, even if I walk through the valley of the shadow of death, I will not be afraid of anything, because You are with me. You have a walking stick with which to guide and one with which to help. These comfort me.

The Lord will always lead you. He will meet the needs of your soul in the dry times and give strength to your body. You will be like a garden that has enough water, like a well of water that never dries up—This is God, our God forever and ever. He will show us the way until death. See, God is honored in His power. Who is a teacher like Him?

Ps.107:7; Deut. 32:10–12—Isa. 46:4; Ps. 23:3–4; Isa. 58:11—Ps. 48:14; Job 36:22.

Open my eyes so that I may see great things from Your Law.

Then He opened their minds to understand the Holy Writings—The Helper is the Holy Spirit. The Father will send Him in My place. He will teach you everything—Whatever is good and perfect comes to us from God. He is the One Who made all light.

I pray that the great God and Father of our Lord Jesus Christ may give you the wisdom of His Spirit. Then you will be able to understand the secrets about Him as you know Him better. I pray that your hearts will be able to understand. I pray that you will know about the hope given by God's call. . . . I pray that you will know how great His power is for those who have put their trust in Him.

LUKE 18:41; PS. 119:18; LUKE 24:45—JOHN 14:26—JAMES 1:17; EPH. 1:17–19.

This is no place of rest—God's people have a complete rest waiting for them—This hope goes into the Holiest Place of All behind the curtain of heaven. Jesus has already gone there. He has become our Religious Leader forever and has made the way for man to go to God.

There are many rooms in My Father's house. If it were not so, I would have told you. I am going away to make a place for you. After I go and make a place for you, I will come back and take you with Me. Then you may be where I am—With Christ, which is much better.

God will take away all their tears. There will be no more death or sorrow or crying or pain. All the old things have passed away—There the troubles of the sinful stop. There the tired are at rest.

Gather together riches in heaven. . . . For wherever your riches are, your heart will be there also—Keep your minds thinking about things in heaven. Do not think about things on the earth.

DEUT. 12:9; MIC. 2:10—HEB. 4:9—HEB. 6:19–20; JOHN 14:2–3—PHIL. 1:23; REV. 21:4—JOB 3:17; MATT. 6:20–21—COL. 3:2.

The pain in death is sin—For then Christ would have had to die many times since the world began. But He came once at the end of the Old Way of Worship. He gave Himself once for all time. He gave Himself to destroy sin. It is in the plan that all men die once. After that, they will stand before God and be judged. It is the same with Christ. He gave Himself once to take away the sins of many. When He comes the second time, He will not need to give Himself again for sin. He will save all those who are waiting for Him.

It is true that we share the same kind of flesh and blood because Jesus became a man like us. He died as we must die. Through His death He destroyed the power of the devil who has the power of death. Jesus did this to make us free from the fear of death. We no longer need to be chained to this fear.

It will soon be time for me to leave this life. I have fought a good fight. I have finished the work I was to do. I have kept the faith. There is a crown which comes from being right with God. The Lord, the One Who will judge, will give it to me on that great day when He comes again.

1 COR. 15:55; 1 COR. 15:56—HEB. 9:26–28; HEB. 2:14–15; 2 TIM. 4:6–8.

They become tired doing so many sins—There is a different law at work deep inside of me that fights with my mind. This law of sin holds me in its power because sin is still in me. There is no happiness in me! Who can set me free from my sinful old self?

Come to Me, all of you who work and have heavy loads. I will give you rest—Now that we have been made right with God by putting our trust in Him, we have peace with Him. It is because of what our Lord Jesus Christ did for us. By putting our trust in God, He has given us His loving-favor and has received us. We are happy for the hope we have of sharing the shining-greatness of God.

The man who goes into God's rest, rests from his own work the same as God rested from His work—I could not be right with God by what the Law said I must do. I was made right with God by faith in Christ— This is the place to rest.

HEB. 4:3; JER. 9:5—ROM. 7:23–24; MATT. 11:28—ROM. 5:1–2; HEB. 4:10—PHIL. 3:9—ISA. 28:12.

If you, Lord, should write down our sins, O Lord, who could stand?—He spoke from his lips without thinking because they went against the Spirit of God.

It is not what goes into a man's mouth that makes his mind and heart sinful. It is what comes out of a man's mouth that makes him sinful.

A bad man spreads trouble. One who hurts people with bad talk separates good friends—There is one whose foolish words cut like a sword, but the tongue of the wise brings healing. Lips that tell the truth will last forever, but a lying tongue lasts only for a little while— But no man can make his tongue say what he wants it to say. It is sinful and does not rest. It is full of poison that kills. Giving thanks and speaking bad words come from the same mouth. My Christian brothers, this is not right!

Put out of your life… anger, bad temper, bad feelings toward others, talk that hurts people, speaking against God, and dirty talk. Do not lie to each other. You have put out of your life your old ways—God wants you to be holy—No lie has come from their mouths.

PS. 141:3; PS. 130:3—PS. 106:33; MATT. 15:11; PROV. 16:28—PROV. 12:18–19—JAMES 3:8, 10; COL. 3:8–9— 1 THESS. 4:3—REV. 14:5.

Let the favor of the Lord our God be upon us.
And make the work of our hands stand strong.

Your name became known among the nations because of your beauty. For it was perfect because of My shining-greatness which I had given to you, says the Lord God— All of us, with no covering on our faces, show the shining-greatness of the Lord as in a mirror. All the time we are being changed to look like Him, with more and more of His shining-greatness. This change is from the Lord Who is the Spirit—The Spirit of shining-greatness and of God is in you.

Happy are all who honor the Lord with fear, and who walk in His ways. For you will eat the fruit of your hands. You will be happy and it will be well with you— Trust your work to the Lord, and your plans will work out well.

You must keep on working to show you have been saved from the punishment of sin. Be afraid that you may not please God. He is working in you. God is helping you obey Him. God is doing what He wants done in you—Our Lord Jesus Christ and God our Father loves us. Through His loving-favor He gives us comfort and hope that lasts forever. May He give your hearts comfort and strength to say and do every good thing.

Ps. 90:17; Ezek. 16:14—2 Cor. 3:18—1 Pet. 4:14; Ps. 128:1-2—Prov. 16:3; Phil. 2:12-13—2 Thess. 2:16-17.

A man who has friends must be a friend, but there is a friend who stays nearer than a brother—The Lord spoke to Moses face to face, as a man speaks to his friend—You are My friends if you do what I tell you. I do not call you servants that I own anymore. A servant does not know what his owner is doing. I call you friends, because I have told you everything I have heard from My Father.

When you do everything you have been told to do, you must say, We are not any special servants. We have done only what we should have done.

You should not act like people who are owned by someone. They are always afraid. Instead, the Holy Spirit makes us His sons, and we can call to Him, My Father.

Learn to pray about everything. Give thanks to God as you ask Him for what you need—The prayer of the faithful is His joy.

MARK 6:30; PROV. 18:24—EXOD. 33:11—JOHN 15:14-15; LUKE 17:10; ROM. 8:15; PHIL. 4:6—PROV. 15:8.

This is what the Lord says: I remember how you loved Me when you were young. Your love was as a bride. I remember how you followed Me in the desert, through a land that had not been planted—I will remember My agreement which I made with you when you were young. And I will make an agreement with you that lasts forever—I will visit you and keep My promise to you. . . . For I know the plans I have for you, says the Lord, plans for well-being and not for trouble, to give you a future and a hope.

For as the heavens are higher than the earth, so are My ways higher than your ways, and My thoughts than your thoughts—I would look to God. I would put my troubles before God. He does great things, too great for us to understand. He does too many wonderful things for us to number—O Lord my God, many are the great works You have done, and Your thoughts toward us. No one can compare with You! If I were to speak and tell of them, there would be too many to number.

NEH. 5:19; JER. 2:2—EZEK. 16:60—JER. 29:10–11; ISA. 55:9—JOB 5:8–9—PS. 40:5.

Every good promise which the Lord had made to the people of Israel came true—God is not a man, that He should lie. He is not a son of man, that He should be sorry for what He has said. Has He said, and will He not do it? Has He spoken, and will He not keep His Word?

The Lord your God is God, the faithful God. He keeps His promise and shows His lovingkindness to those who love Him and keep His Laws—He will remember His agreement forever.

Can a woman forget her nursing child? Can she have no pity on the son to whom she gave birth? Even these may forget, but I will not forget you. See, I have marked your names on My hands.

The Lord your God is with you, a Powerful One Who wins the battle. He will have much joy over you. With His love He will give you new life. He will have joy over you with loud singing.

Josh. 1:5; Josh. 21:45—Num. 23:19; Deut. 7:9—Ps. 111:5; Isa. 49:15–16; Zeph. 3:17.

*Those who know Your name will put their trust in
You. For You, O Lord, have never left alone
those who look for You.*

The name of the Lord is a strong tower. The man who does what is right runs into it and is safe—I will trust and not be afraid. For the Lord God is my strength and song. And He has become the One Who saves me.

I have been young, and now I am old. Yet I have never seen the man who is right with God left alone, or his children begging for bread—For the Lord loves what is fair and right. He does not leave the people alone who belong to Him. They are kept forever. But the children of the sinful will be cut off—The Lord will not leave His people alone, because of His great name. The Lord has been pleased to make you His people—God kept us from what looked like sure death and He is keeping us. As we trust Him, He will keep us in the future.

Be happy with what you have. God has said, I will never leave you or let you be alone. So we can say for sure, The Lord is my Helper. I am not afraid of anything man can do to me.

Ps. 9:10; Prov. 18:10—Isa. 12:2; Ps. 37:25—Ps. 37:28—1 Sam. 12:22—2 Cor. 1:10; Heb. 13:5–6.

Sin will be looked for in Israel, but there will be none. And sin will be looked for in Judah, but it will not be found. For I will forgive those whom I allow to return— Who is a God like You, Who forgives sin and the wrong-doing of Your chosen people who are left? He does not stay angry forever because He is happy to show loving-kindness. He will again have loving-pity on us. He will crush our sins under foot. Yes, You will throw all our sins into the deep sea.

He gave this loving-favor to us through His much-loved Son—Christ can bring you to God, holy and pure and without blame.

There is One Who can keep you from falling and can bring you before Himself free from all sin. He can give you great joy as you stand before Him in His shining-greatness. He is the only God. He is the One Who saves from the punishment of sin through Jesus Christ our Lord. May He have shining-greatness and honor and power and the right to do all things. He had this before the world began, He has it now, and He will have this forever. Let it be so.

REV. 14:5; JER. 50:20—MIC. 7:18–19; EPH. 1:6—COL. 1:22; JUDE 24–25.

You have given a flag to those who fear You, so it may be seen because of the truth.

The Lord is My Banner—When the one who hates us comes in like a flood, the Spirit of the Lord will lift up a wall against him.

We will sing for joy when you win. In the name of our God we will lift up our flags—The Lord has taken our guilt away. Come and let us make the work of the Lord our God known in Zion—We have power over all these things through Jesus Who loves us so much—God is the One Who gives us power over sin through Jesus Christ our Lord. We give thanks to Him for this—Jesus a perfect Leader.

Be strong with the Lord's strength—Lies, and not truth, rule the land—Fight the Lord's battles—Be strong, all you people of the land, says the Lord. Do the work. . . . Do not be afraid—Open your eyes and look at the fields. They are white now and waiting for the grain to be gathered in—In a little while, the One you are looking for will come. It will not be a long time now.

Ps. 60:4; Exod. 17:15—Isa. 59:19; Ps. 20:5—Jer. 51:10—Rom. 8:37—1 Cor. 15:57—Heb. 2:10; Eph. 6:10—Jer. 9:3—1 Sam. 18:17—Hag. 2:4–5—John 4:35—Heb. 10:37.

Many are asking, Who will show us any good? Let the light of Your face shine on us, O Lord. You have filled my heart with more happiness than they have when there is much grain and wine.

As the deer desires rivers of water, so my soul desires You, O God. My soul is thirsty for God, for the living God—O God, You are my God. I will look for You with all my heart and strength. My soul is thirsty for You. My flesh is weak wanting You in a dry and tired land where there is no water.

I am the Bread of Life. He who comes to Me will never be hungry. He who puts his trust in Me will never be thirsty. Sir, give us this Bread all the time—Mary sat at the feet of Jesus and listened to all He said—One thing I have asked from the Lord, that I will look for: that I may live in the house of the Lord all the days of my life, to look upon the beauty of the Lord, and to worship in His holy house.

LUKE 10:42; PS. 4:6–7; PS. 42:1–2—PS. 63:1; JOHN 6:35, 34—LUKE 10:39—PS. 27:4.

May your spirit and your soul and your body be kept complete. May you be without blame when our Lord Jesus Christ comes again.

Christ loved the church. He gave His life for it. Christ did this so the church might stand before Him in shining-greatness. There is to be no sin of any kind in it. It is to be holy and without blame—We preach Christ. We tell every man how he must live. We use wisdom in teaching every man. We do this so every man will be complete in Christ.

The peace of God is much greater than the human mind can understand—Let the peace of Christ have power over your hearts. You were chosen as a part of His body.

Our Lord Jesus Christ and God our Father loves us. Through His loving-favor He gives us comfort and hope that lasts forever. May He give your hearts comfort and strength to say and do every good thing—Christ will keep you strong until He comes again. No blame will be held against you.

1 Thess. 5:23; Eph. 5:25, 27—Col. 1:28; Phil. 4:7—Col. 3:15—2 Thess. 2:16–17—1 Cor. 1:8.

Let them make a holy place for Me, so I may live among them—I will meet there with the people of Israel. It will be set apart by My shining-greatness. I will live among the people of Israel and will be their God.

You have gone up on high. You have taken those who were held with You. You have received gifts of men, even among those who fought against You. So the Lord God may live there with them.

We are the house of the living God. God has said, I will live in them and will walk among them. I will be their God and they will be My people—Your body is a house of God where the Holy Spirit lives—You are also being put together as a part of this building because God lives in you by His Spirit.

The nations will know that I am the Lord Who makes Israel holy, when My holy place is among them forever.

2 CHRON. 6:18; EXOD. 25:8—EXOD. 29:43, 45; PS. 68:18; 2 COR. 6:16—1 COR. 6:19—EPH. 2:22; EZEK. 37:28.

But we know there is only one God. He is the Father. All things are from Him. He made us for Himself. There is one Lord. He is Jesus Christ. He made all things. He keeps us alive—All people will honor the Son as they honor the Father. He who does not honor the Son does not honor the Father Who sent Him—Let us give thanks all the time to God through Jesus Christ. Our gift to Him is to give thanks. Our lips should always give thanks to His name—He who gives a gift of thanks honors Me. And to him who makes his way right, I will show him the saving power of God.

I saw many people. No one could tell how many there were. They were from every nation and from every family and from every kind of people and from every language. They were standing before the throne and before the Lamb. They were wearing white clothes and they held branches in their hands. And they were crying out with a loud voice, We are saved from the punishment of sin by our God Who sits on the throne and by the Lamb! They said, Let it be so! May our God have worship and shining-greatness and wisdom and thanks and honor and power and strength forever. Let it be so!

Ps. 65:1; 1 Cor. 8:6—John 5:23—Heb. 13:15—Ps. 50:23; Rev. 7:9–10, 12.

The One Who saves and makes them free is strong. The Lord of All is His name—I will pay the price to free them from the power of the grave. I will save them from death. O Death, where are your thorns? O Grave, where is your power to destroy?

It is true that we share the same kind of flesh and blood because Jesus became a man like us. He died as we must die. Through His death He destroyed the power of the devil who has the power of death. Jesus did this to make us free from the fear of death. We no longer need to be chained to this fear.

He who puts his trust in the Son has life that lasts forever. He who does not put his trust in the Son will not have life, but the anger of God is on him.

You are dead to the things of this world. Your new life is now hidden in God through Christ. Christ is our life. When He comes again, you will also be with Him to share His shining-greatness—On the day He comes, His shining-greatness will be seen in those who belong to Him.

Ps. 103:4; Jer. 50:34—Hosea 13:14; Heb. 2:14–15; John 3:36; Col. 3:3–4—2 Thess. 1:10.

*He is the only God. He is the One Who saves
from the punishment of sin through
Jesus Christ our Lord.*

God gave us Christ to be our wisdom. Christ made us right with God and set us apart for God and made us holy. Christ bought us with His blood and made us free from our sins—Can you find out the deep things of God? Can you find out how far the All-powerful can go? They are higher than the heavens. What can you do? They are deeper than the place of the dead. What can you know?

What we preach is God's wisdom. It was a secret until now. God planned for us to have this honor before the world began—God kept this secret to Himself from the beginning of the world. And He is the One Who made all things. This was done so the great wisdom of God might be shown now to the leaders and powers in the heavenly places. It is being done through the church.

If you do not have wisdom, ask God for it. He is always ready to give it to you and will never say you are wrong for asking—But the wisdom that comes from heaven is first of all pure. Then it gives peace. It is gentle and willing to obey. It is full of loving-kindness and of doing good. It has no doubts and does not pretend to be something it is not.

JUDE 25; 1 COR. 1:30—JOB 11:7–8; 1 COR. 2:7—EPH. 3:9–10; JAMES 1:5—JAMES 3:17.

Watchman, what is the time of night? The watchman says, The morning comes, but also the night.

In a little while, the One you are looking for will come. It will not be a long time now—He shines on them like the morning light. He is like the sunshine on a morning without clouds.

I am going away to make a place for you. After I go and make a place for you, I will come back and take you with Me. Then you may be where I am. Do not let your hearts be troubled or afraid. You heard Me say that I am going away. But I am coming back to you.

So let all those who hate You die, O Lord. But let those who love Him be like the sun as he rises in his power—For you are children of the light and of the day. We are not of darkness or of night.

There will be no night there.

Job 7:4; Isa. 21:11–12; Heb. 10:37—2 Sam. 23:4; John 14:2–3, 27–28—Judg. 5:31—1 Thess. 5:5; Rev. 21:25.

Give all your cares to the Lord and He will give you strength. He will never let those who are right with Him be shaken—I will trust and not be afraid. For the Lord God is my strength and song. And He has become the One Who saves me.

Why are you afraid? You have so little faith!—Do not worry. Learn to pray about everything. Give thanks to God as you ask Him for what you need. The peace of God is much greater than the human mind can understand. This peace will keep your hearts and minds through Christ Jesus—Your strength will come by being quiet and by trusting.

From the right and good work will come quiet trust forever—Peace I leave with you. My peace I give to you. I do not give peace to you as the world gives. Do not let your hearts be troubled or afraid—May you have loving-favor and peace from God Who was and Who is and Who is to come.

Isa. 26:3; Ps. 55:22—Isa. 12:2; Matt. 8:26—Phil. 4:6–7—Isa. 30:15; Isa. 32:17—John 14:27—Rev. 1:4.

If your brother sins against you, go and tell him what he did without other people hearing it. If he listens to you, you have won your brother back again. . . . Lord, how many times may my brother sin against me and I forgive him, up to seven times? Jesus said to him, I tell you, not seven times but seventy times seven!—When you stand to pray, if you have anything against anyone, forgive him. Then your Father in heaven will forgive your sins also.

God has chosen you. You are holy and loved by Him. Because of this, your new life should be full of loving-pity. You should be kind to others and have no pride. Be gentle and be willing to wait for others. Try to understand other people. Forgive each other. If you have something against someone, forgive him. That is the way the Lord forgave you—You must be kind to each other. Think of the other person. Forgive other people just as God forgave you because of Christ's death on the cross.

The missionaries said to the Lord, Give us more faith.

EPH. 4:26; MATT. 18:15, 21–22—MARK 11:25; COL. 3:12–13—EPH. 4:32; LUKE 17:5.

When you pray, say, Our Father in heaven—My Father and your Father. . .My God and your God!

I am doing what the Father told Me to do—What I say to you, I do not say by My own power. The Father Who lives in Me does His work through Me.

The Father loves the Son and has given all things into His hand—You have given Him power over all men. He is to give life that lasts forever to all You have given to Him.

Lord, show us the Father. That is all we ask. Jesus said to him, Have I been with you all this time and you do not know Me yet? Whoever has seen Me, has seen the Father. How can you say, Show us the Father? Do you not believe that I am in the Father and that the Father is in Me?—My Father and I are one!—I have loved you just as My Father has loved Me. Stay in My love. If you obey My teaching, you will live in My love. In this way, I have obeyed My Father's teaching and live in His love.

JOHN 14:28; LUKE 11:2—JOHN 20:17; JOHN 14:31—
JOHN 14:10—JOHN 3:35—JOHN 17:2; JOHN 14:8–10—
JOHN 10:30—JOHN 15:9–10.

His face was marked worse than any man, and His body more than the sons of men—But He was hurt for our wrongdoing. He was crushed for our sins. He was punished so we would have peace. He was beaten so we would be healed.

Now is the time you are to come and you have come in the dark—You would not have any right or power over Me if it were not given you from above.

The Son of God came to destroy the works of the devil—He put out many demons. Jesus would not allow the demons to speak because they knew Who He was.

All power has been given to Me in heaven and on earth—In My name they will put out demons.

God, Who is our peace, will soon crush Satan under your feet.

GEN. 3:15; ISA. 52:14—ISA. 53:5; LUKE 22:53—JOHN 19:11; 1 JOHN 3:8—MARK 1:34; MATT. 28:18—MARK 16:17; ROM. 16:20.

If then you have been raised with Christ, keep looking for the good things of heaven. This is where Christ is seated on the right side of God. Keep your minds thinking about things in heaven. Do not think about things on the earth. . . . Your new life is now hidden in God through Christ—But we are citizens of heaven. Christ, the One Who saves from the punishment of sin, will be coming down from heaven again. We are waiting for Him to return. He will change these bodies of ours of the earth and make them new. He will make them like His body of shining-greatness. He has the power to do this because He can make all things obey Him.

The things our old selves want to do are against what the Holy Spirit wants. The Holy Spirit does not agree with what our sinful old selves want. These two are against each other. So you cannot do what you want to do—So then, Christian brothers, we are not to do what our sinful old selves want us to do. If you do what your sinful old selves want you to do, you will die in sin. But if, through the power of the Holy Spirit, you destroy those actions to which the body can be led, you will have life—Dear friends, your real home is not here on earth. You are strangers here. I ask you to keep away from all the sinful desires of the flesh. These things fight to get hold of your soul.

Ps. 119:25; Col. 3:1–3—Phil. 3:20–21; Gal. 5:17—Rom. 8:12–13—1 Pet. 2:11.

Someone whose faith is weak—His faith in God was strong, and he gave thanks to God.

You have so little faith! Why did you doubt?—You have much faith. You will have what you asked for.

Do you have faith that I can do this? They said to Him, Yes, Sir! . . . You will have what you want because you have faith.

Give us more faith—You must become strong in your most holy faith—Have your roots planted deep in Christ. Grow in Him. Get your strength from Him. Let Him make you strong in the faith as you have been taught—God is the One Who makes our faith and your faith strong in Christ—After you have suffered for awhile, God Himself will make you perfect. He will keep you in the right way. He will give you strength.

We who have strong faith should help those who are weak. We should not live to please ourselves—So you should stop saying that you think other people are wrong. Instead, decide to live so that your Christian brother will not have a reason to trip or fall into sin because of you.

ROM. 12:3; ROM. 14:1—ROM. 4:20; MATT. 14:31—MATT. 15:28; MATT. 9:28–29; LUKE 17:5—JUDE 20—COL. 2:7— 2 COR. 1:21—1 PET. 5:10; ROM. 15:1—ROM. 14:13.

The Father loves the Son and has given all things into His hand—God lifted Jesus high above everything else. He gave Him a name that is greater than any other name. So when the name of Jesus is spoken, everyone in heaven and on earth and under the earth will bow down before Him. And every tongue will say Jesus Christ is Lord. Everyone will give honor to God the Father—This place was given to Christ. It is much greater than any king or leader can have. No one else can have this place of honor and power. No one in this world or in the world to come can have such honor and power—Christ made everything in the heavens and on the earth. He made everything that is seen and things that are not seen. He made all the powers of heaven. Everything was made by Him and for Him.

Christ died and lived again. This is why He is the Lord of the living and of the dead—When you have Christ, you are complete. He is the head over all leaders and powers—From Him Who has so much we have all received loving-favor, one loving-favor after another.

COL. 1:19; JOHN 3:35—PHIL. 2:9–11—EPH. 1:21—COL. 1:16; ROM. 14:9—COL. 2:10—JOHN 1:16.

Holy men who belonged to God spoke what the Holy Spirit told them—We are preaching what we have heard and seen. We want you to share together with us what we have with the Father and with His Son, Jesus Christ.

Look at My hands and My feet. See! It is I, Myself! Touch Me and see for yourself. A spirit does not have flesh and bones as I have. When Jesus had said this, He showed them His hands and feet—The one who saw it is writing this and what he says is true. He knows he is telling the truth so you may believe.

We had nothing to do with manmade stories when we told you about the power of our Lord Jesus Christ and of His coming again. We have seen His great power with our own eyes—In this way, you do not have faith in Christ because of the wisdom of men. You have faith in Christ because of the power of God.

REV. 1:19; 2 PET. 1:21—1 JOHN 1:3; LUKE 24:39–40—JOHN 19:35; 2 PET. 1:16—1 COR. 2:5.

God has shown His love to us by sending His only Son into the world. God did this so we might have life through Christ. This is love! It is not that we loved God but that He loved us. For God sent His Son to pay for our sins with His own blood.

Who is a God like You, Who forgives sin and the wrong-doing of Your chosen people who are left? He does not stay angry forever because He is happy to show lovingkindness. He will again have loving-pity on us. He will crush our sins under foot. Yes, You will throw all our sins into the deep sea—O Lord my God, I cried to You for help and You healed me. O Lord, You have brought me up from the grave. You have kept me alive, so that I will not go down into the deep—While I was losing all my strength, I remembered the Lord. And my prayer came to You, into Your holy house—I did not give up waiting for the Lord. And He turned to me and heard my cry. He brought me up out of the hole of danger, out of the mud and clay. He set my feet on a rock, making my feet sure.

Isa. 38:17; 1 John 4:9–10; Mic. 7:18–19—Ps. 30:2–3—Jon. 2:7—Ps. 40:1–2.

Now that which we see is as if we were looking in a broken mirror—We do not see all things obey him yet.

All this helps us know that what the early preachers said was true. You will do well to listen to what they have said. Their words are as lights that shine in a dark place. Listen until you understand what they have said. Then it will be like the morning light which takes away the darkness. And the Morning Star (Christ) will rise to shine in your hearts—Your Word is a lamp to my feet and a light to my path.

Dear friends, you must remember the words spoken by the missionaries of our Lord Jesus Christ. They said, In the last days there will be men who will laugh at the truth and will be led by their own sinful desires.—The Holy Spirit tells us in plain words that in the last days some people will turn away from the faith. They will listen to what is said about spirits and follow the teaching about demons.

My children, we are near the end of the world— Night is almost gone. Day is almost here. We must stop doing the sinful things that are done in the dark. We must put on all the things God gives us to fight with for the day.

REV. 1:19; 1 COR. 13:12—HEB. 2:8; 2 PET. 1:19—PS. 119:105—JUDE 17–18—1 TIM. 4:1; 1 JOHN 2:18—ROM. 13:12.

For a little while [Jesus] took a place that was not as important as the angels. But God had loving-favor for everyone. He had Jesus suffer death on a cross for all of us—Christ died for everyone—Adam did not obey God, and many people become sinners through him. Christ obeyed God and makes many people right with Himself.

The first man, Adam, became a living soul. But the last Adam (Christ) is a life-giving Spirit. We have these human bodies first. Then we are given God-like bodies that are ready for heaven—God said, Let Us make man like Us. . . . And God made man in His own likeness. In the likeness of God He made him—God. . .has spoken to us through His Son. . .the shining-greatness of the Father. The Son is as God is in every way—You have given Him power over all men.

Adam was the first man. He was made from the dust of the earth. Christ was the second man. He came down from heaven. All men of the earth are made like Adam. But those who belong to Christ will have a body like the body of Christ Who came from heaven.

ROM. 5:14; HEB. 2:9—2 COR. 5:14—ROM. 5:19; 1 COR. 15:45–46—GEN. 1:26–27—HEB. 1:1–3—JOHN 17:2; 1 COR. 15:47–48.

The Holy Writings say, No eye has ever seen or no ear has ever heard or no mind has ever thought of the wonderful things God has made ready for those who love Him. God has shown these things to us through His Holy Spirit—The Holy Spirit. . .will tell you of things to come.

See! He is coming in the clouds. Every eye will see Him. Even the men who killed Him will see Him. All the people on the earth will cry out in sorrow because of Him. Yes, let it be so.

Christian brothers, we want you to know for sure about those who have died. You have no reason to have sorrow as those who have no hope. We believe that Jesus died and then came to life again. Because we believe this, we know that God will bring to life again all those who belong to Jesus. For the Lord Himself will come down from heaven with a loud call. The head angel will speak with a loud voice. God's horn will give its sounds. First, those who belong to Christ will come out of their graves to meet the Lord. Then, those of us who are still living here on earth will be gathered together with them in the clouds. We will meet the Lord in the sky and be with Him forever.

Rev. 1:19; 1 Cor. 2:9–10—John 16:13; Rev. 1:7; 1 Thess. 4:13–14, 16–17.

Whoever wants to be great among you, let him care for you. Whoever wants to be first among you, let him be your servant. For the Son of Man came not to be cared for. He came to care for others. He came to give His life so that many could be bought by His blood and made free from the punishment of sin.

If anyone thinks he is important when he is nothing, he is fooling himself—God has given me His loving-favor. This helps me write these things to you. I ask each one of you not to think more of himself than he should think. Instead, think in the right way toward yourself by the faith God has given you—When you do everything you have been told to do, you must say, We are not any special servants. We have done only what we should have done.

I am happy to say this. Whatever we did in this world, and for sure when we were with you, we were honest and had pure desires. We did not trust in human wisdom. Our power came from God's loving-favor—We have this light from God in our human bodies. This shows that the power is from God. It is not from ourselves.

ACTS 20:19; MATT. 20:26–28; GAL. 6:3—ROM. 12:3— LUKE 17:10—2 COR. 1:12; 2 COR. 4:7.

Noah. . .planted a grape-field. And he drank of the wine, and drank too much—When he was about to go into Egypt, Abram said to his wife Sarai, . . .Say that you are my sister. Then it may go well with me because of you—Isaac said to Jacob, . . .Is it true that you are my son Esau? Jacob answered, I am—Moses. . .spoke from his lips without thinking—The men of Israel took some of their food. They did not ask the Lord what they should do. Joshua made peace with them—David did what was right in the eyes of the Lord. He did not turn away from anything the Lord told him to do all the days of his life, except in what happened with Uriah the Hittite.

It was because of their faith that God was pleased with them—Anyone can be made right with God by the free gift of His lovingfavor. It is Jesus Christ Who bought them with His blood and made them free from their sins—All of us like sheep have gone the wrong way. Each of us has turned to his own way. And the Lord has put on Him the sin of us all.

I want you to know that I am not doing this because of you, says the Lord God. Be ashamed and troubled because of your ways, O people of Israel!

Isa. 53:6; Gen. 9:20–21—Gen. 12:11, 13—Gen. 27:21, 24—Ps. 106:32–33—Josh. 9:14–15—1 Kings 15:5; Heb. 11:39—Rom. 3:24—Isa. 53:6; Ezek. 36:32.

Christ became human flesh and lived among us. We saw His shining-greatness. This greatness is given only to a much-loved Son from His Father. He was full of loving-favor and truth—You have honored Your Word because of what Your name is.

They will give Him the name Immanuel. This means God with us—You will give Him the name Jesus because He will save His people from the punishment of their sins.

He does this so that all people will honor the Son as they honor the Father—God lifted Jesus high above everything else. He gave Him a name that is greater than any other name—This place was given to Christ. It is much greater than any king or leader can have. No one else can have this place of honor and power. No one in this world or in the world to come can have such honor and power. God has put all things under Christ's power and has made Him to be the head leader over all things of the church—His name is written on Him but He is the only One Who knows what it says. . .KING OF KINGS AND LORD OF LORDS.

We cannot come near the All-powerful—What is His name, and what is His Son's name? For sure you know!

Isa. 9:6; John 1:14—Ps. 138:2; Matt. 1:23— Matt. 1:21; John 5:23—Phil. 2:9—Eph. 1:21–22—Rev. 19:12, 16; Job 37:23—Prov. 30:4.

You belong to Christ, and Christ belongs to God—I am my love's, and he wants me—I am his—The Son of God. . .loved me and gave Himself for me.

You do not belong to yourselves. God bought you with a great price. So honor God with your body. You belong to Him—But the Lord has taken you and brought you out of the iron stove, out of Egypt, to be His own people, as you are this day.

You are God's field. You are God's building also—Christ was faithful as a Son Who is Head of God's house. We are of God's house if we keep our trust in the Lord until the end. This is our hope—You are to be as living stones in the building God is making also. You are His religious leaders giving yourselves to God through Jesus Christ.

They will be Mine says the Lord of All, on that day that I gather My special people—All that is Mine is Yours. All that is Yours is Mine. I have been honored through them—I pray that you will see how great the things are that He has promised to those who belong to Him.

DEUT. 32:9; 1 COR. 3:23—SONG OF SOL. 7:10—SONG OF SOL. 2:16—GAL. 2:20; 1 COR. 6:19–20—DEUT. 4:20; 1 COR. 3:9—HEB. 3:6—1 PET. 2:5; MAL. 3:17—JOHN 17:10; EPH. 1:18.

*Any branch that gives fruit, He cuts it
back so it will give more fruit.*

He is like a fire for making gold pure, and like a strong
cleaner. He will sit as one who melts silver and makes it
pure. He will make the sons of Levi pure. He will make
them pure like gold and silver, so that they may bring the
right gifts to the Lord.

We are glad for our troubles also. We know that
troubles help us learn not to give up. When we have
learned not to give up, it shows we have stood the test.
When we have stood the test, it gives us hope. Hope
never makes us ashamed because the love of God has
come into our hearts through the Holy Spirit Who was
given to us—Do not give up when you are punished by
God. Be willing to take it, knowing that God is teaching
you as a son. Is there a father who does not punish his
son sometimes? If you are not punished as all sons are, it
means that you are not a true son of God. You are not a
part of His family and He is not your Father. There is no
joy while we are being punished. It is hard to take, but
later we can see that good came from it. And it gives us
the peace of being right with God. So lift up your hands
that have been weak. Stand up on your weak legs.

John 15:2; Mal. 3:2–3; Rom. 5:3–5—Heb. 12:7–8,
11–12.

44

For the high and honored One Who lives forever, Whose name is Holy, says, I live in the high and holy place. And I also live with those who are sorry for their sins and have turned from them and are not proud. I give new strength to the spirit of those without pride, and also to those whose hearts are sorry for their sins.

It is better to be poor in spirit among poor people, than to divide the riches that were taken with the proud—Those who know there is nothing good in themselves are happy, because the holy nation of heaven is theirs.

There are six things which the Lord hates, yes, seven that are hated by Him: A proud look, a lying tongue, and hands that kill those who are without guilt—Everyone who is proud in heart is a shame to the Lord. For sure, that one will be punished.

Look into me, O God, and know my heart. Try me and know my thoughts. See if there is any sinful way in me and lead me in the way that lasts forever.

May you have loving-favor and peace from God our Father and the Lord Jesus Christ. I thank God for you whenever I think of you—Those who have no pride in their hearts are happy, because the earth will be given to them.

MAL. 3:15; ISA. 57:15; PROV. 16:19—MATT. 5:3; PROV. 6:16–17—PROV. 16:5; PS. 139:23–24; PHIL. 1:2–3— MATT. 5:5.

O Lord, You are my God. I will praise You. I will give thanks to Your name. For You have been faithful to do great things, plans that You made long ago—The Lord is all that I am to receive, and my cup.

He makes me strong again. He leads me in the way of living right with Himself which brings honor to His name. Yes, even if I walk through the valley of the shadow of death, I will not be afraid of anything, because You are with me. You have a walking stick with which to guide and one with which to help. These comfort me—Yet I am always with You. You hold me by my right hand. You will lead me by telling me what I should do. And after this, You will bring me into shining-greatness. Whom have I in heaven but You? I want nothing more on earth, but You. My body and my heart may grow weak, but God is the strength of my heart and all I need forever—For our heart is full of joy in Him, because we trust in His holy name—The Lord will finish the work He started for me. O Lord, Your loving-kindness lasts forever. Do not turn away from the works of Your hands.

Ps. 48:14; Isa. 25:1—Ps. 16:5; Ps. 23:3–4—Ps. 73:23–26—Ps. 33:21—Ps. 138:8.

I call to You from the end of the earth when my heart is weak. Lead me to the rock that is higher than I.

My eyes are tired from looking up. O Lord, I am having a hard time. Keep me safe—Give all your cares to the Lord and He will give you strength.

Now, O Lord my God, You have made Your servant king in place of my father David. But I am only a little child. I do not know how to start or finish—If you do not have wisdom, ask God for it. He is always ready to give it to you and will never say you are wrong for asking.

Who is able for such a work?—I know there is nothing good in me, that is, in my flesh—I am all you need. I give you My loving-favor. My power works best in weak people.

Son, take hope. Your sins are forgiven. Daughter, take hope! Your faith has healed you.

My soul will be filled as with rich foods. . . . On my bed I remember You. I think of You through the hours of the night.

PS. 94:19; PS. 61:2; ISA. 38:14—PS. 55:22; 1 KINGS 3:7—JAMES 1:5; 2 COR. 2:16—ROM. 7:18—2 COR. 12:9; MATT. 9:2, 22; PS. 63:5–6.

I am the Lord. Those who wait for Me with hope will not be put to shame—Good will come to the man who trusts in the Lord, and whose hope is in the Lord—You will keep the man in perfect peace whose mind is kept on You, because he trusts in You. Trust in the Lord forever. For the Lord God is a Rock that lasts forever—My soul is quiet and waits for God alone. My hope comes from Him—I am not ashamed. I know the One in Whom I have put my trust.

God made a promise. He wanted to show Abraham that He would never change His mind. So He made the promise in His own name. God gave these two things that cannot be changed and God cannot lie. We who have turned to Him can have great comfort knowing that He will do what He has promised. This hope is a safe anchor for our souls. It will never move. This hope goes into the Holiest Place of All behind the curtain of heaven. Jesus has already gone there. He has become our Religious Leader forever and has made the way for man to go to God.

Rom. 5:5; Isa. 49:23—Jer. 17:7—Isa. 26:3–4—Ps. 62:56—2 Tim. 1:12—Heb. 6:17–20.

If anyone wants to be My follower, he must forget about himself. He must take up his cross and follow Me.

Do you not know that to love the sinful things of the world and to be a friend to them is to be against God? Yes, I say it again, if you are a friend of the world, you are against God—We must suffer many hard things to get into the holy nation of God.

The person who puts his trust in the Rock (Christ) will not be put to shame—This Stone is of great worth to you who have your trust in Him. But to those who have not put their trust in Him, the Holy Writings say, The Stone which the workmen put aside has become the most important part of the building. The Holy Writings say, also, Christ is the Stone that some men will trip over and the Rock over which they will fall.

I do not want to be proud of anything except in the cross of our Lord Jesus Christ. Because of the cross, the ways of this world are dead to me, and I am dead to them— I have been put up on the cross to die with Christ—Those of us who belong to Christ have nailed our sinful old selves on His cross. Our sinful desires are now dead.

If we suffer and stay true to Him, then we will be a leader with Him. If we say we do not know Him, He will say He does not know us.

GAL. 5:11; MATT. 16:24; JAMES 4:4—ACTS 14:22; ROM. 9:33—1 PET. 2:7–8; GAL. 6:14—GAL. 2:20—GAL. 5:24; 2 TIM. 2:12.

For the Lord Himself will come down from heaven with a loud call. The head angel will speak with a loud voice. God's horn will give its sounds. First, those who belong to Christ will come out of their graves to meet the Lord. Then, those of us who are still living here on earth will be gathered together with them in the clouds. We will meet the Lord in the sky and be with Him forever. Because of this, comfort each other with these words— He Who tells these things says, Yes, I am coming soon! Let it be so. Come, Lord Jesus.

Dear friends, since you are waiting for these things to happen, do all you can to be found by Him in peace. Be clean and free from sin—Keep away from everything that even looks like sin. May the God of peace set you apart for Himself. May every part of you be set apart for God. May your spirit and your soul and your body be kept complete. May you be without blame when our Lord Jesus Christ comes again. The One Who called you is faithful and will do what He promised.

You must be willing to wait also. Be strong in your hearts because the Lord is coming again soon.

PHIL. 4:5; 1 THESS. 4:16–18—REV. 22:20; 2 PET. 3:14— 1 THESS. 5:22–24; JAMES 5:8.

Let me sing for my loved one a love song about His grape-field: My loved one had a grape-field on a hill that grows much fruit. He dug all around it and took away its stones, and planted it with the best vine. . . . Then He expected it to give good grapes, but it gave only wild grapes—Yet I planted you as a vine of much worth, in every way a true seed. How then have you turned away from Me and become a wild vine?

The things your sinful old self wants to do are: sex sins, sinful desires, wild living, . . .wanting something someone else has, killing other people, using strong drink, wild parties, and all things like these. . . . But the fruit that comes from having the Holy Spirit in our lives is: love, joy, peace, not giving up, being kind, being good, having faith, being gentle, and being the boss over our own desires.

I am the true Vine. My Father is the One Who cares for the Vine. He takes away any branch in Me that does not give fruit. Any branch that gives fruit, He cuts it back so it will give more fruit. Get your life from Me and I will live in you. No branch can give fruit by itself. It has to get life from the vine. You are able to give fruit only when you have life from Me. When you give much fruit, My Father is honored. This shows you are My followers.

GEN. 49:11; ISA. 5:1–2—JER. 2:21; GAL. 5:19, 21–23; JOHN 15:1–2, 4, 8.

Men become right with God by putting their trust in Jesus Christ. God will accept men if they come this way.

Christ never sinned but God put our sin on Him. Then we are made right with God because of what Christ has done for us—Christ bought us with His blood and made us free from the Law—God gave us Christ to be our wisdom. Christ made us right with God and set us apart for God and made us holy. Christ bought us with His blood and made us free from our sins—It was not because we worked to be right with God. It was because of His loving-kindness that He washed our sins away. At the same time He gave us new life when the Holy Spirit came into our lives. God gave the Holy Spirit to fill our lives through Jesus Christ, the One Who saves.

It is so much better to know Christ Jesus my Lord. I have lost everything for Him. And I think of these things as worth nothing so that I can have Christ. I want to be as one with Him. I could not be right with God by what the Law said I must do. I was made right with God by faith in Christ.

Rom. 3:22; 2 Cor. 5:21—Gal. 3:13—1 Cor. 1:30—Titus 3:5–6—Phil. 3:8–9.

Jesus. . .looked up to heaven and said, Father. . .Holy Father—He said, Father—Because you are the sons of God, He has sent the Spirit of His Son into our hearts. The Spirit cries, Father!—Now all of us can go to the Father through Christ by way of the one Holy Spirit. From now on you are not strangers and people who are not citizens. You are citizens together with those who belong to God. You belong in God's family.

You are our Father. . . . You, O Lord, are our Father. The One Who bought us and made us free from long ago is Your name.

I will get up and go to my father. I will say to him, Father, I have sinned against heaven and against you. I am not good enough to be called your son. But may I be as one of the workmen you pay to work? The son got up and went to his father. While he was yet a long way off, his father saw him. The father was full of loving-pity for him. He ran and threw his arms around him and kissed him.

Do as God would do. Muchloved children want to do as their fathers do.

ROM. 8:15; JOHN 17:1, 11—MARK 14:36—GAL. 4:6—
EPH. 2:18–19; ISA. 63:16; LUKE 15:18–20; EPH. 5:1.

So let us go to Him outside the city to share His shame.
For there is no city here on earth that will last forever.
We are looking for the one that is coming.

Dear friends, your faith is going to be tested as if it were going through fire. Do not be surprised at this. Be happy that you are able to share some of the suffering of Christ. When His shining-greatness is shown, you will be filled with much joy—Our hope for you is the same all the time. We know you are sharing our troubles. And so you will share the comfort we receive.

If men speak bad of you because you are a Christian, you will be happy because the Spirit of shining-greatness and of God is in you.

The missionaries went away from the court happy that they could suffer shame because of His Name—He chose to suffer with God's people instead of having fun doing sinful things for awhile. Any shame that he suffered for Christ was worth more than all the riches in Egypt. He kept his eyes on the reward God was going to give him.

HEB. 13:13–14; 1 PET. 4:12–13—2 COR. 1:7; 1 PET. 4:14; ACTS 5:41—HEB. 11:25–26.

> *Christ...will change these bodies of ours of the earth and make them new. He will make them like His body of shining-greatness.*

Above the large covering that was over their heads there was something that looked like a throne, and looked like it was made of sapphire. Sitting on the throne was what looked like a man. Then I saw that there was something like shining brass from the center of his body and up to his head. It looked like fire all around within it. And from the center of his body and down to his feet I saw something like fire. There was a bright light shining all around Him. This light shining around Him looked like the rainbow in the clouds on a day of rain. This was what the shining-greatness of the Lord looked like.

All of us, with no covering on our faces, show the shining-greatness of the Lord as in a mirror. All the time we are being changed to look like Him, with more and more of His shining-greatness. This change is from the Lord Who is the Spirit—It has not yet been shown to us what we are going to be. We know that when He comes again, we will be like Him because we will see Him as He is.

They will never be hungry or thirsty again—They were singing the song of Moses, who was a servant owned by God, and the song of the Lamb.

PHIL. 3:20–21; EZEK. 1:26–28; 2 COR. 3:18—1 JOHN 3:2; REV. 7:16—REV. 15:3.

In these last days [God] has spoken to us through His Son. . . . The Son shines with the shining-greatness of the Father. The Son is as God is in every way. It is the Son Who holds up the whole world by the power of His Word. The Son gave His own life so we could be clean from all sin. After He had done that, He sat down on the right side of God in heaven—Christ never sinned but God put our sin on Him. Then we are made right with God because of what Christ has done for us.

Be sure you honor Him with love and fear all the days of your life here on earth. You know you were not bought and made free from sin by paying gold or silver. . . . The blood of Christ saved you. This blood is of great worth and no amount of money can buy it. Christ was given as a lamb without sin and without spot. Long before the world was made, God chose Christ to be given to you in these last days—For the love of Christ puts us into action. We are sure that Christ died for everyone. So, because of that, everyone has a part in His death. Christ died for everyone so that they would live for Him. They should not live to please themselves but for Christ Who died on a cross and was raised from the dead for them.

1 John 3:5; Heb. 1:2–3—2 Cor. 5:21; 1 Pet. 1:17–20—2 Cor. 5:14–15.

For I am not pleased with the death of anyone who dies, says the Lord God. So be sorry for your sins and turn away from them, and live.

I have come and have spoken to them so they are guilty of sin. But now they have no reason to give for keeping their sin any longer.

The servant who knew what the owner wanted done, but did not get ready for him, or did not do what he wanted done, will be beaten many times.

You get what is coming to you when you sin. It is death! But God's free gift is life that lasts forever. It is given to us by our Lord Jesus Christ—He who puts his trust in the Son has life that lasts forever. He who does not put his trust in the Son will not have life, but the anger of God is on him—Do you not know that when you give yourself as a servant to be owned by someone, that one becomes your owner? If you give yourself to sin, the end is death. If you give yourself to God, the end is being right with Him.

If anyone wants to serve Me, he must follow Me. So where I am, the one who wants to serve Me will be there also. If anyone serves Me, My Father will honor him.

DEUT. 30:19; EZEK. 18:32; JOHN 15:22; LUKE 12:47; ROM. 6:23—JOHN 3:36—ROM. 6:16; JOHN 12:26.

When you are put into their hands, do not be afraid of what you are to say or how you are to say it. Whatever is given to you to say at that time, say it. It will not be you who speaks, but the Holy Spirit—Do not worry about tomorrow. Tomorrow will have its own worries. The troubles we have in a day are enough for one day.

The God of Israel Himself gives strength and power to His people. Honor and thanks be to God!—He gives strength to the weak. And He gives power to him who has little strength.

I am all you need. I give you My loving-favor. My power works best in weak people. I am happy to be weak and have troubles so I can have Christ's power in me. I receive joy when I am weak. I receive joy when people talk against me and make it hard for me and try to hurt me and make trouble for me. I receive joy when all these things come to me because of Christ. For when I am weak, then I am strong—I can do all things because Christ gives me the strength—O my soul, walk on with strength.

Deut. 33:25; Mark 13:11—Matt. 6:34; Ps. 68:35—Isa. 40:29; 2 Cor. 12:9–10—Phil. 4:13—Judg. 5:21.

There is no joy while we are being punished. It is hard to take, but later we can see that good came from it. And it gives us the peace of being right with God—the fruit that comes from having the Holy Spirit in our lives.

You moved them out with Your strong wind on the day of the east wind.

The Lord has loving-pity on those who fear Him, as a father has loving-pity on his children.

Our human body is wearing out. But our spirits are getting stronger every day. The little troubles we suffer now for a short time are making us ready for the great things God is going to give us forever. We do not look at the things that can be seen. We look at the things that cannot be seen. The things that can be seen will come to an end. But the things that cannot be seen will last forever.

Our Religious Leader understands how weak we are. Christ was tempted in every way we are tempted, but He did not sin.

SONG OF SOL. 4:16; HEB. 12:11—GAL. 5:22; ISA. 27:8; Ps. 103:13; 2 COR. 4:16–18; HEB. 4:15.

O Lord, You have looked through me and have known me. You know when I sit down and when I get up. You understand my thoughts from far away. You look over my path and my lying down. You know all my ways very well. Even before I speak a word, O Lord, You know it all. All You know is too great for me. It is too much for me to understand.

The eyes of the Lord are in every place, watching the bad and the good—The ways of a man are seen by the eyes of the Lord, and He watches all his paths—You are the kind of people who make yourselves look good before other people. God knows your hearts. What men think is good is hated in the eyes of God—The eyes of the Lord move over all the earth so that He may give strength to those whose whole heart is given to Him.

Jesus...did not need anyone to tell Him about man. He knew what was in man—Lord, You know everything. You know I love You.

GEN. 16:13; PS. 139:1–4, 6; PROV. 15:3—PROV. 5:21—LUKE 16:15—2 CHRON. 16:9; JOHN 2:24–25—JOHN 21:17.

O Lord my God, I will give thanks to You with all my heart. I will bring honor to Your name forever.

He who gives a gift of thanks honors Me—It is good to give thanks to the Lord, and sing praises to Your name, O Most High. It is good to tell of Your loving-kindness in the morning, and of how faithful You are at night.

Let everything that has breath praise the Lord.

Christian brothers, I ask you...to give your bodies to God because of His loving-kindness to us. Let your bodies be a living and holy gift given to God. He is pleased with this kind of gift. This is the true worship that you should give Him—Jesus...suffered and died outside the city so His blood would make the people clean from sin. Let us give thanks all the time to God through Jesus Christ. Our gift to Him is to give thanks. Our lips should always give thanks to His name—Always give thanks for all things to God the Father in the name of our Lord Jesus Christ

The Lamb Who was killed has the right to receive power and riches and wisdom and strength and honor and shining-greatness and thanks.

Ps. 86:12; Ps. 50:23—Ps. 92:1-2; Ps. 150:6; Rom. 12:1—Heb. 13:12, 15—Eph. 5:20; Rev. 5:12.

> *Let us keep running in the race that God has planned for us. Let us keep looking to Jesus. Our faith comes from Him and He is the One Who makes it perfect.*

If anyone wants to follow Me, he must give up himself and his own desires. He must take up his cross everyday and follow Me—Whoever does not give up all that he has, cannot be My follower—We must stop doing the sinful things that are done in the dark.

Everyone who runs in a race does many things so his body will be strong. He does it to get a prize that will soon be worth nothing, but we work for a prize that will last forever. In the same way, I run straight for the place at the end of the race. I fight to win. I do not beat the air. I keep working over my body. I make it obey me. I do this because I am afraid that after I have preached the Good News to others, I myself might be put aside— No, Christian brothers, I do not have that life yet. But I do one thing. I forget everything that is behind me and look forward to that which is ahead of me. My eyes are on the prize. I want to win the race and get the prize of God's call from heaven through Christ Jesus—So keep on trying to know the Lord.

Heb. 12:1–2; Luke 9:23—Luke 14:33—Rom. 13:12; 1 Cor. 9:25–27—Phil. 3:13–14—Hosea 6:3.

Bring up a child by teaching him the way he should go, and when he is old he will not turn away from it.

Remember that our fathers on earth punished us. We had respect for them. How much more should we obey our Father in heaven and live? For a little while our fathers on earth punished us when they thought they should. But God punishes us for our good so we will be holy as He is holy.

Before I suffered I went the wrong way, but now I obey Your Word. It is good for me that I was troubled, so that I might learn Your Law.

I know the plans I have for you, says the Lord, plans for well-being and not for trouble, to give you a future and a hope—So put away all pride from yourselves. You are standing under the powerful hand of God. At the right time He will lift you up.

Lam. 3:27; Prov. 22:6; Heb. 12:9–10; Ps. 119:67, 71; Jer. 29:11—1 Pet. 5:6.

Drive out the people who live in the land in front of you. If you do not, then those who are allowed to stay will be like sharp pieces in your eyes and like thorns in your sides. They will trouble you in the land where you live.

Fight the good fight of faith—We do not use those things to fight with that the world uses. We use the things God gives to fight with and they have power. Those things God gives to fight with destroy the strong-places of the devil. We break down every thought and proud thing that puts itself up against the wisdom of God. We take hold of every thought and make it obey Christ.

So then, Christian brothers, we are not to do what our sinful old selves want us to do. If you do what your sinful old selves want you to do, you will die in sin. But if, through the power of the Holy Spirit, you destroy those actions to which the body can be led, you will have life.

The things our old selves want to do are against what the Holy Spirit wants. The Holy Spirit does not agree with what our sinful old selves want. These two are against each other. So you cannot do what you want to do—There is a different law at work deep inside of me that fights with my mind. This law of sin holds me in its power because sin is still in me—But we have power over all these things through Jesus Who loves us so much.

NUM. 33:55; 1 TIM. 6:12—2 COR. 10:4–5; ROM. 8:12–13; GAL. 5:17—ROM. 7:23—ROM. 8:37.

If anyone does sin, there is One Who will go between him and the Father. He is Jesus Christ, the One Who is right with God. He paid for our sins with His own blood. He did not pay for ours only, but for the sins of the whole world—God gave Jesus Christ to the world. Men's sins can be forgiven through the blood of Christ when they put their trust in Him. God gave His Son Jesus Christ to show how right He is. Before this, God did not look on the sins that were done. But now God proves that He is right in saving men from sin. He shows that He is the One Who has no sin. God makes anyone right with Himself who puts his trust in Jesus.

Let him be kind to him, and say, Save him from going down to the grave. I have found someone to pay the price to make him free.

What can we say about all these things? Since God is for us, who can be against us? Who can say anything against the people God has chosen? It is God Who says they are right with Himself. Who then can say we are guilty? It was Christ Jesus Who died. He was raised from the dead. He is on the right side of God praying to Him for us.

1 SAM. 2:25; 1 JOHN 2:1–2—ROM. 3:25–26; JOB 33:24; ROM. 8:31, 33–34.

Our life is lived by faith. We do not live by what we see in front of us—We love Him because He loved us first—We have come to know and believe the love God has for us. God is love. If you live in love, you live by the help of God and God lives in you—The truth is the Good News. When you heard the truth, you put your trust in Christ. Then God marked you by giving you His Holy Spirit as a promise—God wants these great riches of the hidden truth to be made known to the people who are not Jews. The secret is this: Christ in you brings hope of all the great things to come.

If a person says, I love God, but hates his brother, he is a liar. If a person does not love his brother whom he has seen, how can he love God Whom he has not seen?

Jesus said to him, Thomas, because you have seen Me, you believe. Those are happy who have never seen Me and yet believe!—Happy are all who put their trust in Him.

1 Pet. 1:8; 2 Cor. 5:7—1 John 4:19—1 John 4:16—Eph. 1:13—Col. 1:27; 1 John 4:20; John 20:29—Ps. 2:12.

All of us have become like one who is unclean. All our right and good works are like dirty pieces of cloth.

I will have much joy in the Lord. My soul will have joy in my God, for He has clothed me with the clothes of His saving power. He has put around me a coat of what is right and good, as a man at his own wedding wears something special on his head, and as a bride makes herself beautiful with stones of great worth.

Get the best coat and put it on him—She was given clean, white, fine linen clothes to wear. The fine linen is the right living of God's people.

I think of everything as worth nothing. It is so much better to know Christ Jesus my Lord. I have lost everything for Him. And I think of these things as worth nothing so that I can have Christ. I want to be as one with Him. I could not be right with God by what the Law said I must do. I was made right with God by faith in Christ.

Jer. 23:6; Isa. 64:6; Isa. 61:10; Luke 15:22—Rev. 19:8; Phil. 3:8–9.

Why are you sleeping? Get up and pray that you will not be tempted—Man's spirit is willing, but the body does not have the power to do it.

Two things I have asked of You. Do not keep me from having them before I die: Take lies and what is false far from me. Do not let me be poor or rich. Feed me with the food that I need. Then I will not be afraid that I will be full and turn my back against You and say, Who is the Lord? And I will not be afraid that I will be poor and steal, and bring shame on the name of my God.

The Lord will keep you from all that is sinful. He will watch over your soul—I will take you from the hand of the sinful. And I will free you from the hand of those who would hurt you—We know that no child of God keeps on sinning. The Son of God watches over him and the devil cannot get near him

I will keep you from the time of trouble. The time to test everyone is about to come to the whole world. I will do this because you have listened to Me and have waited long and have not given up—The Lord knows how to help men who are right with God when they are tempted.

1 CHRON. 4:10; LUKE 22:46—MATT. 26:41; PROV. 30:7-9; PS. 121:7—JER. 15:21—1 JOHN 5:18; REV. 3:10—2 PET. 2:9.

They had been arguing along the road about who was the greatest. Jesus sat down and called the followers to Him. He said, If anyone wants to be first, he must be last of all. He will be the one to care for all—Be gentle as you care for each other. God works against those who have pride. He gives His loving-favor to those who do not try to honor themselves. So put away all pride from yourselves. You are standing under the powerful hand of God. At the right time He will lift you up.

Think as Christ Jesus thought. . . . He did not hold to His rights as God. He put aside everything that belonged to Him and made Himself the same as a servant who is owned by someone. He became human by being born as a man. Because of this, God lifted Jesus high above everything else. He gave Him a name that is greater than any other name. So when the name of Jesus is spoken, everyone in heaven and on earth and under the earth will bow down before Him.

Those who are wise will shine like the bright heavens. And those who lead many to do what is right and good will shine like the stars forever and ever.

1 Cor. 15:41; Mark 9:34–35—1 Pet. 5:5–6; Phil. 2:5–7, 9–10; Dan. 12:3.

Be strong.... Do the work, for I am with you, says the Lord of All.

I am the Vine and you are the branches. Get your life from Me. Then I will live in you and you will give much fruit. You can do nothing without Me—I can do all things because Christ gives me the strength—Be strong with the Lord's strength—The joy of the Lord is your strength.

You who are now listening to these words spoken through the men of God who were there when the Lord's house was started, let your hands be strong for building the Lord's house—Give strength to weak hands and to weak knees. Say to those whose heart is afraid, Have strength of heart, and do not be afraid— The Lord looked at him and said, Go in this strength of yours.

Since God is for us, who can be against us?— Through God's loving-kindness, He has given us this job to do. So we do not give up.

Do not let yourselves get tired of doing good. If we do not give up, we will get what is coming to us at the right time—God is the One Who gives us power over sin through Jesus Christ our Lord. We give thanks to Him for this.

HAG. 2:4; JOHN 15:5—PHIL. 4:13—EPH. 6:10—NEH. 8:10; ZECH. 8:9—ISA. 35:3–4—JUDG. 6:14; ROM. 8:31—2 COR. 4:1; GAL. 6:9—1 COR. 15:57.

God's eyes are upon the ways of a man, and He sees all his steps. There is no darkness or shadow where sinners can hide themselves—Can a man hide himself in secret places so that I cannot see him? says the Lord. Do I not fill heaven and earth? says the Lord.

You will not be afraid of trouble at night. . . . You will not be afraid of the sickness that walks in darkness. Because you have made the Lord your safe place, and the Most High the place where you live, nothing will hurt you. No trouble will come near your tent—He Who watches over you will not sleep. The Lord watches over you. The Lord is your safe cover at your right hand. The sun will not hurt you during the day and the moon will not hurt you during the night. The Lord will keep you from all that is sinful. He will watch over your soul.

Yes, even if I walk through the valley of the shadow of death, I will not be afraid of anything, because You are with me.

Ps. 139:12; Job 34:21–22—Jer. 23:24; Ps. 91:5–6, 9–10—Ps. 121:3, 5–7; Ps. 23:4.

They did not think about the country they had come from. If they had, they might have gone back. But they wanted a better country. And so God is not ashamed to be called their God. He has made a city for them. He chose to suffer with God's people instead of having fun doing sinful things for awhile. Any shame that he suffered for Christ was worth more than all the riches in Egypt—For the one right with God lives by faith. If anyone turns back, I will not be pleased with him. We are not of those people who turn back and are lost. Instead, we have faith to be saved from the punishment of sin—Anyone who puts his hand on a plow and looks back at the things behind is of no use in the holy nation of God.

I do not want to be proud of anything except in the cross of our Lord Jesus Christ. Because of the cross, the ways of this world are dead to me, and I am dead to them—Come out from among them. Do not be joined to them. Touch nothing that is sinful. And I will receive you.

I am sure that God Who began the good work in you will keep on working in you until the day Jesus Christ comes again.

DEUT. 17:16; HEB. 11:15–16, 25–26—HEB. 10:38–39—
LUKE 9:62; GAL. 6:14—2 COR. 6:17; PHIL. 1:6.

When I was only a little angry, they added to the trouble.

Christian brothers, if a person is found doing some sin, you who are stronger Christians should lead that one back into the right way. Do not be proud as you do it. Watch yourself, because you may be tempted also.

If he turns a sinner from the wrong way, he will save the sinner's soul from death and many sins will be forgiven—Comfort those who feel they cannot keep going on. Help the weak. Understand and be willing to wait for all men.

So you should stop saying that you think other people are wrong. Instead, decide to live so that your Christian brother will not have a reason to trip or fall into sin because of you—We who have strong faith should help those who are weak. We should not live to please ourselves.

Love is not happy with sin—The person who thinks he can stand against sin had better watch that he does not fall into sin.

Ps. 69:26; Zech. 1:15; Gal. 6:1; James 5:20—1 Thess. 5:14; Rom. 14:13—Rom. 15:1; 1 Cor. 13:6—1 Cor. 10:12.

The day you eat from it you will die for sure—She took of its fruit and ate. She also gave some to her husband, and he ate.

You get what is coming to you when you sin. It is death! But God's free gift is life that lasts forever. It is given to us by our Lord Jesus Christ—The power of death was over all men because of the sin of one man, Adam. But many people will receive His loving-favor and the gift of being made right with God. They will have power in life by Jesus Christ—Death came because of a man, Adam. Being raised from the dead also came because of a Man, Christ. All men will die as Adam died. But all those who belong to Christ will be raised to new life—Jesus Christ, the One Who saves... He put a stop to the power of death and brought life that never dies which is seen through the Good News.

God gave us life that lasts forever, and this life is in His Son. He that has the Son has life. He that does not have the Son of God does not have life—For God did not send His Son into the world to say it is guilty. He sent His Son so the world might be saved from the punishment of sin by Him.

John 10:10; Gen. 2:17—Gen. 3:6; Rom. 6:23—Rom. 5:17—1 Cor. 15:21–22—2 Tim. 1:10; 1 John 5:11–12—John 3:17.

You know of the loving-favor shown by our Lord Jesus Christ. He was rich, but He became poor for your good. In that way, because He became poor, you might become rich—Sin spread when the Law was given. But where sin spread, God's loving-favor spread all the more.

He did this to show us through all the time to come the great riches of His loving-favor. He has shown us His kindness through Christ Jesus. It is not given to you because you worked for it. If you could work for it, you would be proud—We know we cannot become right with God by obeying the Law. A man is made right with God by putting his trust in Jesus Christ. For that reason, we have put our trust in Jesus Christ also. We have been made right with God because of our faith in Christ and not by obeying the Law. No man can be made right with God by obeying the Law—It was because of His loving-kindness that He washed our sins away. At the same time He gave us new life when the Holy Spirit came into our lives. God gave the Holy Spirit to fill our lives through Jesus Christ, the One Who saves.

1 TIM. 1:14; 2 COR. 8:9—ROM. 5:20; EPH. 2:7, 9—GAL. 2:16—TITUS 3:5–6.

A star will come out of Jacob—Night is almost gone. Day is almost here. We must stop doing the sinful things that are done in the dark. We must put on all the things God gives us to fight with for the day—Until the morning comes and the shadows hurry away, turn, my love. Be like a gazelle or a young deer on the mountains of Bether.

Watchman, what is the time of night? Watchman, what is the time of night? The watchman says, The morning comes, but also the night. If you have questions to ask, ask them, and come back again.

I am the Light of the world—And I will give him the Morning Star.

Be careful! Watch and pray. You do not know when it will happen. The coming of the Son of Man is as a man who went from his house to a far country. He gave each one of his servants some work to do. He told the one standing at the door to watch. In the same way, you are to watch also! . . . He may come when you are not looking for Him and find you sleeping. What I say to you, I say to all. Watch!

REV. 22:16; NUM. 24:17—ROM. 13:12—SONG OF SOL. 2:17; ISA. 21:11–12; JOHN 8:12—REV. 2:28; MARK 13:33–37.

*When you have eaten and are filled,
you will honor and thank the Lord your
God for the good land He has given you.*

Be careful not to forget the Lord your God by not keeping all His Laws which I am telling you today— One of them turned back when he saw he was healed. He thanked God with a loud voice. He got down on his face at the feet of Jesus and thanked Him. He was from the country of Samaria. Jesus asked, Were there not ten men who were healed? Where are the other nine? Is this stranger from another country the only one who turned back to give thanks to God?

Everything God made is good. We should not put anything aside if we can take it and thank God for it. It is made holy by the Word of God and prayer—The man who eats meat does it to honor the Lord. He gives thanks to God for what he eats—The good that comes from the Lord makes one rich, and He adds no sorrow to it.

Praise the Lord, O my soul. And all that is within me, praise His holy name. Praise the Lord, O my soul. . . . He forgives all my sins. . . . He crowns me with lovingkindness and pity.

DEUT. 8:10; DEUT. 8:11—LUKE 17:15–18: 1 TIM. 4:4–5—ROM. 14:6—PROV. 10:22; PS. 103:1–4.

Jesus Christ is the same yesterday and today and forever—Our Religious Leader understands how weak we are. Christ was tempted in every way we are tempted, but He did not sin—He knows how to be gentle with those who know little. He knows how to help those who are doing wrong—Jesus came to the followers and found them sleeping. He said to Peter, Simon, are you sleeping? Were you not able to watch one hour? Watch and pray so that you will not be tempted. Man's spirit wants to do this, but the body does not have the power to do it.

The Lord has loving-pity on those who fear Him, as a father has loving-pity on his children. For He knows what we are made of. He remembers that we are dust.

But You, O Lord, are a God full of love and pity. You are slow to anger and rich in loving-kindness and truth. Turn to me, and show me loving-kindness. Give Your strength to Your servant. And save the son of your woman servant.

MATT. 14:14; HEB. 13:8—HEB. 4:15—HEB. 5:2—MARK 14:37–38; Ps. 103:13–14; Ps. 86:15–16.

I do not call you servants that I own anymore.
A servant does not know what his owner is doing.
I call you friends, because I have told you everything
I have heard from My Father.

The Lord said, Should I hide from Abraham what I am about to do. . . ?—You were given the secrets about the holy nation of heaven—God has shown these things to us through His Holy Spirit. It is the Holy Spirit Who looks into all things, even the secrets of God, and shows them to us—It was a secret until now. God planned for us to have this honor before the world began.

Happy is the man You choose and bring near to You to live in Your holy place. We will be filled with the good things of Your house, Your holy house—The secret of the Lord is for those who fear Him. And He will make them know His agreement—I gave them the Word which You gave Me. They received it. They know I came from You and they believe You sent Me.

You are My friends if you do what I tell you.

JOHN 15:15; GEN. 18:17—MATT. 13:11—1 COR. 2:10—1 COR. 2:7; PS. 65:4—PS. 25:14—JOHN 17:8; JOHN 15:14.

The walls were on twelve stones. The names of the twelve missionaries of the Lamb were written on the stones.

From now on you are not strangers and people who are not citizens. You are citizens together with those who belong to God. You belong in God's family. This family is built on the teachings of the missionaries and the early preachers. Jesus Christ Himself is the cornerstone, which is the most important part of the building. Christ keeps this building together and it is growing into a holy building for the Lord. You are also being put together as a part of this building because God lives in you by His Spirit—If you have tasted of the Lord, you know how good He is. Come to Christ as to a living stone. Men have put Him aside, but He was chosen by God and is of great worth in the sight of God. You are to be as living stones in the building God is making also. You are His religious leaders giving yourselves to God through Jesus Christ. This kind of gift pleases God.

All will be quiet before You, and praise belongs to You, O God, in Zion.

Isa. 60:18; Rev. 21:14; Eph. 2:19–22—1 Pet. 2:3–5; Ps. 65:1.

Your sun will set no more, and your moon will not become less. For the Lord will be your light forever and ever, and the days of your sorrow will end—He will take away death for all time. The Lord God will dry tears from all faces. He will take away the shame of His people from all the earth—These are the ones who came out of the time of much trouble. They have washed their clothes and have made them white in the blood of the Lamb. For this reason they are before the throne of God. They help Him day and night in the house of God. And He Who sits on the throne will care for them as He is among them. They will never be hungry or thirsty again. The sun or any burning heat will not shine down on them. For the Lamb Who is in the center of the throne will be their Shepherd. He will lead them to wells of the water of life—God will take away all their tears. There will be no more death or sorrow or crying or pain. All the old things have passed away.

Luke 16:25; Isa. 60:20—Isa. 25:8—Rev. 7:14–17—Rev. 21:4.

From now on those who are dead who died belonging to the Lord will be happy. . . . They will have rest from all their work. All the good things they have done will follow them—There the troubles of the sinful stop. There the tired are at rest—Samuel said to Saul, Why have you troubled my rest by bringing me up?

Whatever your hand finds to do, do it with all your strength. For there is no work or planning or learning or wisdom in the place of the dead where you are going—The dead do not praise the Lord. Neither do those who go down into the quiet place.

It will soon be time for me to leave this life. I have fought a good fight. I have finished the work I was to do. I have kept the faith. There is a crown which comes from being right with God. The Lord, the One Who will judge, will give it to me on that great day when He comes again.

And so God's people have a complete rest waiting for them. The man who goes into God's rest, rests from his own work the same as God rested from His work.

JOHN 9:4; REV. 14:13—JOB 3:17—1 SAM. 28:15; ECCLES. 9:10—PS. 115:17; 2 TIM. 4:6–8; HEB. 4:9–10.

But the person who is not a Christian does not understand these words from the Holy Spirit. He thinks they are foolish. He cannot understand them because he does not have the Holy Spirit to help him understand—Open my eyes so that I may see great things from Your Law.

Jesus spoke to all the people, saying, I am the Light of the world. Anyone who follows Me will not walk in darkness. He will have the Light of Life—All of us, with no covering on our faces, show the shining-greatness of the Lord as in a mirror. All the time we are being changed to look like Him, with more and more of His shining-greatness. This change is from the Lord Who is the Spirit—It was God Who said, The light will shine in darkness. (Genesis 1:3) He is the One Who made His light shine in our hearts. This brings us the light of knowing God's shining-greatness which is seen in Christ's face.

I pray that the great God and Father of our Lord Jesus Christ may give you the wisdom of His Spirit. Then you will be able to understand the secrets about Him as you know Him better. I pray that your hearts will be able to understand. I pray that you will know about the hope given by God's call. I pray that you will see how great the things are that He has promised to those who belong to Him.

LUKE 11:34; 1 COR. 2:14—PS. 119:18; JOHN 8:12— 2 COR. 3:18—2 COR. 4:6; EPH. 1:17–18.

Our early fathers. . .all walked from the country of Egypt under the cloud that showed them the way, and they all passed through the waters of the Red Sea. They were all baptized as they followed Moses in the cloud and in the sea. All of them ate the same holy food. They all drank the same holy drink. They drank from a holy Rock that went along with them. That holy Rock was Christ— One of the soldiers pushed a spear into His side. Blood and water ran out—He was hurt for our wrongdoing. He was crushed for our sins. He was punished so we would have peace. He was beaten so we would be healed.

You do not want to come to Me so you might have life—My people have done two sinful things: They have turned away from Me, the well of living waters. And they have cut out of the rock wells for water for themselves. They are broken wells that cannot hold water.

If anyone is thirsty, let him come to Me and drink— Let the one who wants to drink of the water of life, drink it. It is a free gift.

Ps. 78:20; 1 Cor. 10:1–4—John 19:34—Isa. 53:5; John 5:40—Jer. 2:13; John 7:37—Rev. 22:17.

Those who feared the Lord spoke often to one another, and the Lord listened to them. And the names of those who worshiped the Lord and honored Him were written down before Him in a Book to be remembered.

While they were talking together, Jesus Himself came and walked along with them—For where two or three are gathered together in My name, there I am with them—There are others who worked with me. Their names are in the book of life.

Let the teaching of Christ and His words keep on living in you. These make your lives rich and full of wisdom. Keep on teaching and helping each other. Sing the Songs of David and the church songs and the songs of heaven with hearts full of thanks to God—Help each other. Speak day after day to each other while it is still today so your heart will not become hard by being fooled by sin.

On the day men stand before God, they will have to give an answer for every word they have spoken that was not important. For it is by your words that you will not be guilty and it is by your words that you will be guilty—See, it is written before Me.

MAL. 3:16; LUKE 24:15—MATT. 18:20—PHIL. 4:3; COL. 3:16—HEB. 3:13; MATT. 12:36–37—ISA. 65:6.

I will be to Israel like the water on the grass in the early morning. He will grow like the lily, and have roots like the cedars of Lebanon. His young branches will spread out and his beauty will be like the olive tree. His smell will be like the cedars of Lebanon—Good will come to the man who trusts in the Lord, and whose hope is in the Lord. He will be like a tree planted by the water, that sends out its roots by the river. It will not be afraid when the heat comes but its leaves will be green. It will not be troubled in a dry year, or stop giving fruit.

I am the Lord. I bring down the high tree and make the low tree grow tall. I dry up the green tree, and make the dry tree become green.

The man who is right and good will grow like the palm tree. He will grow like a tall tree in Lebanon. Planted in the house of the Lord, they will grow well in the home of our God. They will still give fruit when they are old. They will be full of life and strength.

Ps. 104:16; Hosea 14:5–6—Jer. 17:7–8; Ezek. 17:24; Ps. 92:12–14.

I have made Your name known to the people You have given Me from the world. They were Yours but You gave them to Me. They have obeyed Your Word. I pray for them. I do not pray for the world. I pray for those You gave Me. They are Yours. All that is Mine is Yours. All that is Yours is Mine. I have been honored through them. Father, I want My followers You gave Me to be with Me where I am. Then they may see My shining-greatness which You gave Me because You loved Me before the world was made.

I will come back and take you with Me. Then you may be where I am—On the day He comes, His shining-greatness will be seen in those who belong to Him—Those of us who are still living here on earth will be gathered together with them in the clouds. We will meet the Lord in the sky and be with Him forever—You will be a crown of beauty in the hand of the Lord, a king's crown in the hand of your God.

MAL. 3:17; JOHN 17:6, 9–10, 24; JOHN 14:3—2 THESS. 1:10—1 THESS. 4:17—ISA. 62:3.

It was God Who said, The light will shine in darkness. (Genesis 1:3) He is the One Who made His light shine in our hearts. This brings us the light of knowing God's shining-greatness which is seen in Christ's face—Christ became human flesh and lived among us. We saw His shining-greatness. This greatness is given only to a much-loved Son from His Father. He was full of loving-favor and truth. The much-loved Son is beside the Father. No man has ever seen God. But Christ has made God known to us.

My soul is thirsty for God, for the living God. When will I come and meet with God?—You have said, Look for My face. My heart said to You, O Lord, Your face will I look for.

All of us, with no covering on our faces, show the shining-greatness of the Lord as in a mirror. All the time we are being changed to look like Him, with more and more of His shining-greatness. This change is from the Lord Who is the Spirit—Father, I want My followers You gave Me to be with Me where I am. Then they may see My shining-greatness which You gave Me because You loved Me before the world was made.

EXOD. 33:18; 2 COR. 4:6—JOHN 1:14, 18; PS. 42:2—PS. 27:8; 2 COR. 3:18—JOHN 17:24.

There is one Man standing between God and men. That Man is Christ Jesus—He became human by being born as a man. After He became a man, He gave up His important place and obeyed by dying on a cross—It is true that we share the same kind of flesh and blood because Jesus became a man like us. He died as we must die. Through His death He destroyed the power of the devil who has the power of death.

I am the Living One. I was dead, but look, I am alive forever—We know that Christ was raised from the dead. He will never die again. Death has no more power over Him. He died once but now lives. He died to break the power of sin, and the life He now lives is for God— Then what would you say if you saw the Son of Man going up where He was before?—It is the same power that raised Christ from the dead. This same power put Christ at God's right side in heaven—Christ is not only God-like, He is God in human flesh.

Christ's weak human body died on a cross. It is by God's power that Christ lives today. We are weak. We are as He was. But we will be alive with Christ through the power God has for us.

EZEK. 1:26; 1 TIM. 2:5—PHIL. 2:7-8—HEB. 2:14; REV. 1:18—ROM. 6:9-10—JOHN 6:62—EPH. 1:20—COL. 2:9; 2 COR. 13:4.

The first man, Adam, became a living soul. But the last Adam (Christ) is a life-giving Spirit.

The Father has life in Himself. He has given power to the Son to have life in Himself—I am the One Who raises the dead and gives them life. Anyone who puts his trust in Me will live again, even if he dies. Anyone who lives and has put his trust in Me will never die. Do you believe this?

Life began by Him. His Life was the Light for men. He gave the right and the power to become children of God to those who received Him. He gave this to those who put their trust in His name. These children of God were not born of blood and of flesh and of man's desires, but they were born of God.

It is the Spirit that gives life. The flesh is of no help. The words I speak to you are spirit and life—God's Word is living and powerful. It is sharper than a sword that cuts both ways. It cuts straight into where the soul and spirit meet and it divides them. It cuts into the joints and bones. It tells what the heart is thinking about and what it wants to do.

Ps. 119:50; 1 Cor. 15:45; John 5:26—John 11:25–26; John 1:4, 12–13—John 6:63—Heb. 4:12.

I am happy to do Your will, O my God. Your Law is within my heart.

Do not think that I have come to do away with the Law of Moses or the writings of the early preachers. I have not come to do away with them but to complete them. I tell you, as long as heaven and earth last, not one small mark or part of a word will pass away of the Law of Moses until it has all been done—Because He is right and good, the Lord was pleased to make the Law great and give it honor—Unless you are more right with God than the teachers of the Law and the proud religious law-keepers, you will never get into the holy nation of heaven.

The Law could not make me free from the power of sin and death. It was weak because it had to work with weak human beings. But God sent His own Son. He came to earth in a body of flesh which could be tempted to sin as we in our bodies can be. He gave Himself to take away sin. By doing that, He took away the power sin had over us. In that way, Jesus did for us what the Law said had to be done. We do not do what our sinful old selves tell us to do anymore. Now we do what the Holy Spirit wants us to do—Christ has put an end to the Law, so everyone who has put his trust in Christ is made right with God.

MATT. 3:15; PS. 40:8; MATT. 5:17–18—ISA. 42:21—MATT. 5:20; ROM. 8:3–4—ROM. 10:4.

Whom have I in heaven but You? I want nothing more on earth, but You. My body and my heart may grow weak, but God is the strength of my heart and all I need forever—The Lord is all that I am to receive, and my cup. My future is in Your hands. The land given to me is good. Yes, my share is beautiful to me.

The Lord is my share, says my soul, so I have hope in Him.

I have been given Your Law forever. It is the joy of my heart.

O God, You are my God. I will look for You with all my heart and strength. My soul is thirsty for You. My flesh is weak wanting You in a dry and tired land where there is no water. For You have been my help. And I sing for joy in the shadow of Your wings.

My love is mine, and I am his.

NUM. 18:20; Ps. 73:25–26—Ps. 16:5–6; LAM. 3:24; Ps. 119:111; Ps. 63:1, 7; SONG OF SOL. 2:16.

The Lord has looked down from heaven on the sons of men, to see if there are any who understand and look for God. They have all turned aside. Together they have become bad. There is no one who does good, not even one—Those who do what their sinful old selves want to do cannot please God.

I know there is nothing good in me, that is, in my flesh. For I want to do good but I do not. I do not do the good I want to do. Instead, I am always doing the sinful things I do not want to do—All of us have become like one who is unclean. All our right and good works are like dirty pieces of cloth. And all of us dry up like a leaf. Our sins take us away like the wind.

But the Holy Writings say that all men are guilty of sin. Then that which was promised might be given to those who put their trust in Christ. It will be because their faith is in Him—God was in Christ. He was working through Christ to bring the whole world back to Himself. God no longer held men's sins against them.

If we say that we have no sin, we lie to ourselves and the truth is not in us. If we tell Him our sins, He is faithful and we can depend on Him to forgive us of our sins. He will make our lives clean from all sin.

PROV. 20:9; PS. 14:2–3—ROM. 8:8; ROM. 7:18–19—ISA. 64:6; GAL. 3:22—2 COR. 5:19; 1 JOHN 1:8–9.

The Lord on high is more powerful than the sound of many waters and the strong waves of the sea—Lord God of all, powerful Lord, who is like You? All around You we see how faithful You are. You rule over the rising sea. When its waves rise, You quiet them.

Do you not fear Me? says the Lord. Do you not shake in fear before Me? For I have placed the sand to be on one side of the sea, a lasting wall that it cannot cross.

When you pass through the waters, I will be with you. When you pass through the rivers, they will not flow over you.

Peter got out of the boat and walked on the water to Jesus. But when he saw the strong wind, he was afraid. He began to go down in the water. He cried out, Lord, save me! At once Jesus put out His hand and took hold of him. Jesus said to Peter, You have so little faith! Why did you doubt?

When I am afraid, I will trust in You.

Ps. 93:3; Ps. 93:4—Ps. 89:8–9; Jer. 5:22; Isa. 43:2; Matt. 14:29–31; Ps. 56:3.

Live with love as Christ loved you. He gave Himself for us, a gift on the altar to God which was as a sweet smell to God—This Stone is of great worth to you who have your trust in Him—God lifted Jesus high above everything else. He gave Him a name that is greater than any other name. So when the name of Jesus is spoken, everyone in heaven and on earth and under the earth will bow down before Him—For Christ is not only God-like, He is God in human flesh.

If you love Me, you will do what I say—The love of God has come into our hearts through the Holy Spirit Who was given to us—The house was filled with the smell of the special perfume—They were surprised and wondered how easy it was for Peter and John to speak. They could tell they were men who had not gone to school. But they knew they had been with Jesus.

O Lord, our Lord, how great is Your name in all the earth. You have set Your shining-greatness above the heavens—Immanuel. This means God with us—For to us a Child will be born. To us a Son will be given. And the rule of the nations will be on His shoulders. His name will be called Wonderful, Teacher, Powerful God, Father Who Lives Forever, Prince of Peace—The name of the Lord is a strong tower. The man who does what is right runs into it and is safe.

SONG OF SOL. 1:3; EPH. 5:2—1 PET. 2:7—PHIL. 2:9–10—COL. 2:9; JOHN 14:15—ROM. 5:5—JOHN 12:3—ACTS 4:13; PS. 8:1—MATT. 1:23—ISA. 9:6—PROV. 18:10.

See, a son will be born to you, who will be a man of peace. I will give him peace from all those who hate him on every side. His name will be Solomon. And I will give peace and quiet to Israel in his days.

See, Someone greater than Solomon is here!—For to us a Child will be born. To us a Son will be given. And the rule of the nations will be on His shoulders. His name will be called Wonderful, Teacher, Powerful God, Father Who Lives Forever, Prince of Peace—Then my people will live in a place of peace, in safe homes, and in quiet resting places. But it will hail when the many trees come down and all the city will be laid waste.

We have peace because of Christ—He will be their peace. When the Assyrian comes into our land. . . .

These kings will fight and make war with the Lamb. But the Lamb will win the war because He is Lord of lords and King of kings.

Peace I leave with you. My peace I give to you.

JUDG. 6:24; 1 CHRON. 22:9; MATT. 12:42—ISA. 9:6—ISA. 32:18–19; EPH. 2:14—MIC. 5:5; REV 17:14; JOHN 14:27.

Lord, all my desire is before You. And my breathing deep within is not hidden from You. . . . For my sins are gone over my head. Like a heavy load, they weigh too much for me—Who can set me free from my sinful old self?

Everything on the earth cries out with pain the same as a woman giving birth to a child. . . . The Holy Spirit is the first of God's gifts to us. . . . We are waiting to become His complete sons when our bodies are made free—You need to have sorrow and all kinds of tests for awhile. I know that I will soon be leaving this body—Our human bodies made from dust must be changed into a body that cannot be destroyed. Our human bodies that can die must be changed into bodies that will never die. When this that can be destroyed has been changed into that which cannot be destroyed, and when this that does die has been changed into that which cannot die, then it will happen as the Holy Writings said it would happen. They said, Death has no more power over life.

2 Cor. 5:4; Ps. 38:9; Ps 38:4—Rom. 7:24; Rom. 8:22–23—1 Pet. 1:6; 2 Pet. 1:14—1 Cor. 15:53-54.

The rest of the bull, he is to bring to a clean place away from the tents, where the ashes are poured out. There he will burn it on wood with fire.

They took Jesus and led Him away. Jesus carried His own cross to a hill called the Place of the Skull. There they nailed Him to the cross—The head religious leader takes the blood of animals into the holy place to give it on the altar for sins. But the bodies of the animals are burned outside the city. It was the same with Jesus. He suffered and died outside the city so His blood would make the people clean from sin. So let us go to Him outside the city to share His shame—I want to understand and have a share in His sufferings.

Be happy that you are able to share some of the suffering of Christ. When His shining-greatness is shown, you will be filled with much joy—The little troubles we suffer now for a short time are making us ready for the great things God is going to give us forever.

LEV. 4:12; JOHN 19:16–18—HEB. 13:11–13—PHIL. 3:10; I PET. 4:13—2 COR. 4:17.

If we are God's children, we should not think of Him as being like gold or silver or stone. Such gods made of gold or silver or stone are planned by men and are made by them.

But God had so much loving-kindness. He loved us with such a great love. Even when we were dead because of our sins, He made us alive by what Christ did for us. We are His work. He has made us to belong to Christ Jesus so we can work for Him. He planned that we should do this—God knew from the beginning who would put their trust in Him. So He chose them and made them to be like His Son. Christ was first and all those who belong to God are His brothers.

We know that when He comes again, we will be like Him because we will see Him as He is—I will be happy to see You when I awake.

He who has power and wins will receive these things. I will be his God and he will be My son—If we are children of God, we will receive everything He has promised us. We will share with Christ all the things God has given to Him.

GEN. 1:27; ACTS 17:29; EPH. 2:4–5, 10—ROM. 8:29; 1 JOHN 3:2—PS. 17:15; REV. 21:7—ROM. 8:17.

Many are asking, Who will show us any good? Let the light of Your face shine on us, O Lord—I will sing of Your strength. Yes, I will sing with joy of Your loving-kindness in the morning. For You have been a strong and safe place for me in times of trouble.

As for me, when all was going well, I said, I will never be moved. . . . But when You hid Your face, I was troubled. I cried to You, O Lord. I begged the Lord for loving-kindness. What good will come from my blood, if I go down to the grave? Will the dust thank You? Will it tell how You are faithful? Hear, O Lord. And show me loving-kindness. O Lord, be my Helper.

For a short time I left you, but with much loving pity I will take you back. When I was very angry I hid My face from you for a short time. But with loving-kindness that lasts forever I will have pity on you, says the Lord Who bought you and saves you—Sorrow will turn into joy—Crying may last for a night, but joy comes with the new day.

JER. 17:17; Ps. 4:6—Ps. 59:16; Ps. 30:6–10; ISA. 54:7–8—JOHN 16:20—Ps. 30:5.

Who can make clean what is unclean?—See, I was born in sin and was in sin from my very beginning.

Dead because of your sins. . . We were sinful from birth like all other people and would suffer from the anger of God—I am not my own boss. Sin is my boss. I do not understand myself. I want to do what is right but I do not do it. Instead, I do the very thing I hate. I know there is nothing good in me, that is, in my flesh.

Sin came into the world by one man, Adam. . . . Adam did not obey God, and many people become sinners through him—Many people died because of the sin of this one man, Adam. But the loving-favor of God came to many people also. This gift came also by one Man Jesus Christ, God's Son.

The power of the Holy Spirit has made me free from the power of sin and death. This power is mine because I belong to Christ Jesus.

But God is the One Who gives us power over sin through Jesus Christ our Lord. We give thanks to Him for this.

GEN. 5:3; JOB 14:4—PS. 51:5; EPH. 2:1, 3—ROM. 7:14–15, 18; ROM. 5:12, 19—ROM. 5:15; ROM. 8:2; I COR. 15:57.

For the Lord gives wisdom. Much learning and understanding come from His mouth.

Trust in the Lord with all your heart, and do not trust in your own understanding—If you do not have wisdom, ask God for it. He is always ready to give it to you and will never say you are wrong for asking—God's plan looked foolish to men, but it is wiser than the best plans of men. God's plan which may look weak is stronger than the strongest plans of men—But God has chosen what the world calls foolish to shame the wise. In that way, no man can be proud as he stands before God.

The opening up of Your Word gives light. It gives understanding to the child-like—Your Word have I hid in my heart, that I may not sin against You.

They all spoke well of Jesus and agreed with the words He spoke—No man has ever spoken like this Man speaks—God gave us Christ to be our wisdom. Christ made us right with God and set us apart for God and made us holy.

PROV. 2:6; PROV. 3:5—JAMES 1:5—1 COR. 1:25—1 COR. 1:27, 29; PS. 119:130—PS. 119:11; LUKE 4:22—JOHN 7:46—1 COR. 1:30.

You will honor the fiftieth year as holy. And let it be known in all the land that all who are living there are free. It will be a happy time for you. Each of you will return to what is his. . .to his family.

Your dead will live. Their dead bodies will rise. You who lie in the dust, wake up and call out for joy. For as the water on the grass in the morning brings new life, the earth will bring back to life those who have been dead.

For the Lord Himself will come down from heaven with a loud call. The head angel will speak with a loud voice. God's horn will give its sounds. First, those who belong to Christ will come out of their graves to meet the Lord. Then, those of us who are still living here on earth will be gathered together with them in the clouds. We will meet the Lord in the sky and be with Him forever.

I will pay the price to free them from the power of the grave. I will save them from death. O Death, where are your thorns? O Grave, where is your power to destroy? I will have no loving-pity.

The One Who saves and makes them free is strong. The Lord of All is His name.

Isa. 63:4; Lev. 25:10; Isa. 26:19; 1 Thess. 4:16–17; Hosea 13:14; Jer. 50:34.

He will see what the suffering of His soul brings, and will be pleased.

Jesus. . .said, It is finished. He put His head down and gave up His spirit—Christ never sinned but God put our sin on Him. Then we are made right with God because of what Christ has done for us.

The people whom I made for Myself will make known My praise—This was done so the great wisdom of God might be shown now to the leaders and powers in the heavenly places. It is being done through the church. This was the plan God had for all time. He did this through Christ Jesus our Lord—He did this to show us through all the time to come the great riches of His loving-favor. He has shown us His kindness through Christ Jesus.

You put your trust in Christ. Then God marked you by giving you His Holy Spirit as a promise. . .that we will receive everything God has for us. . .until God finishes His work of making us complete. . .to show His shining-greatness—But you are a chosen group of people. . . religious leaders. . .a holy nation. You belong to God. He has done this for you so you can tell others how God has called you out of darkness into His great light.

Isa. 53:11; John 19:30—2 Cor. 5:21; Isa. 43:21—Eph. 3:10–11—Eph. 2:7; Eph. 1:13–14—1 Pet. 2:9.

When you are tempted to do wrong, do not say, God is tempting me. God cannot be tempted. He will never tempt anyone. A man is tempted to do wrong when he lets himself be led by what his bad thoughts tell him to do. . . . When sin completes its work, it brings death.

They wanted many things in the desert, and they tempted God there.

Jesus was full of the Holy Spirit. . . . Then He was led by the Holy Spirit to a desert. He was tempted by the devil for forty days and He ate nothing during that time. After that He was hungry. The devil said to Him, If You are the Son of God, tell this stone to be made into bread.

Because Jesus was tempted as we are and suffered as we do, He understands us and He is able to help us when we are tempted—Simon, Simon, listen! Satan has wanted to have you. He will divide you as wheat is divided from that which is no good. But I have prayed for you. . .that your faith will be strong and that you will not give up.

HEB. 3:8; JAMES 1:13–15; PS. 106:14; LUKE 4:1–3; HEB. 2:18—LUKE 22:31–32.

I am the Lord your God, Who has set you apart from all other peoples. Be holy to Me, for I the Lord am holy. I have divided you from the nations, so you belong to Me.

You who have been chosen by God the Father— Make them holy for Yourself by the truth. Your Word is truth—May the God of peace set you apart for Himself .... May your spirit and your soul and your body be kept complete. . .without blame when our Lord Jesus Christ comes again.

Jesus. . .suffered and died outside the city so His blood would make the people clean from sin—Christ Jesus. . .gave Himself for us. He did this by buying us with His blood and making us free from all sin. He gave Himself so His people could be clean and want to do good—Both Jesus and the ones being made holy have the same Father. That is why Jesus is not ashamed to call them His brothers—I set Myself apart to be holy for them. Then they may be made holy by the truth—set apart for holy living by the Holy Spirit. May you obey Jesus Christ and be made clean by His blood.

LEV. 20:8; LEV. 20:24, 26; JUDE 1—JOHN 17:17—1 THESS. 5:23; HEB. 13:12—TITUS 2:13–14—HEB. 2:11—JOHN 17:19—1 PET. 1:2.

*Light is spread like seed for those who are right
and good, and joy for the pure in heart.*

Those who plant with tears will gather fruit with songs of joy. He who goes out crying as he carries his bag of seed will return with songs of joy as he brings much grain with him.

When you put it in the earth, you are not planting the body which it will become. You put in only a seed.

Let us thank the God and Father of our Lord Jesus Christ. It was through His loving-kindness that we were born again to a new life and have a hope that never dies. This hope is ours because Jesus was raised from the dead. With this hope you can be happy even if you need to have sorrow and all kinds of tests for awhile. These tests have come to prove your faith and to show that it is good. Gold, which can be destroyed, is tested by fire. Your faith is worth much more than gold and it must be tested also. Then your faith will bring thanks and shining-greatness and honor to Jesus Christ when He comes again.

Ps. 97:11; Ps. 126:5–6; 1 Cor. 15:37; 1 Pet. 1:3, 6–7.

Who is the man who fears the Lord?
He will teach him in the way he should choose.

The eye is the light of the body. If your eye is good, your whole body will be full of light.

Your Word is a lamp to my feet and a light to my path—Your ears will hear a word behind you, saying, This is the way, walk in it, whenever you turn to the right or to the left—I will show you and teach you in the way you should go. I will tell you what to do with My eye upon you. Do not be like the horse or the donkey which have no understanding. They must be made to work by using bits and leather ropes or they will not come to you. Many are the sorrows of the sinful. But loving-kindness will be all around the man who trusts in the Lord. Be glad in the Lord and be full of joy, you who are right with God! Sing for joy all you who are pure in heart!

O Lord, I know that a man's way is not known by himself. It is not in man to lead his own steps.

Ps. 25:12; Matt. 6:22; Ps. 119:105—Isa. 30:21—Ps. 32:8–11; Jer. 10:23.

> *You will not be afraid when you lie down.*
> *When you lie down, your sleep will be sweet.*

A bad wind storm came up. The waves were coming over the side of the boat. It was filling up with water. Jesus was in the back part of the boat sleeping on a pillow.

Do not worry. Learn to pray about everything. Give thanks to God as you ask Him for what you need. The peace of God is much greater than the human mind can understand. This peace will keep your hearts and minds through Christ Jesus.

I will lie down and sleep in peace. O Lord, You alone keep me safe—For the Lord gives to His loved ones even while they sleep.

While they threw stones at Stephen, he prayed, Lord Jesus, receive my spirit. After that he fell on his knees and cried out with a loud voice, Lord, do not hold this sin against them. When he had said this, he died—free of these bodies. . .at home with the Lord.

PROV. 3:24; MARK 4:37–38; PHIL. 4:6–7; PS. 4:8—PS. 127:2; ACTS 7:59–60—2 COR. 5:8.

See! The Lamb of God Who takes away the sin of the world!—The Lamb Who was killed—The blood of animals cannot take away the sins of men. When Christ came to the world, He said to God, You do not want animals killed or gifts given in worship. You have made My body ready to give as a gift. Our sins are washed away and we are made clean because Christ gave His own body as a gift to God. He did this once for all time.

Abel brought a gift of the first-born of his flocks and of the fat parts. The Lord showed favor to Abel and his gift—Christ loved you. He gave Himself for us, a gift on the altar to God which was as a sweet smell to God.

Let us come near to God with a true heart full of faith. Our hearts must be made clean from guilty feelings and our bodies washed with pure water—Now we know we can go into the Holiest Place of All because the blood of Jesus was given.

HEB. 12:24; JOHN 1:29—REV. 13:8—HEB. 10:4–5, 10; GEN. 4:4—EPH. 5:2—HEB. 10:22—HEB. 10:19.

From noon until three o'clock it was dark over all the land. About three o'clock Jesus cried with a loud voice, My God, My God, why have You left Me alone?—The Lord has put on Him the sin of us all.

Those who belong to Christ will not suffer the punishment of sin—We have been made right with God by putting our trust in Him, we have peace with Him. . .because of. . .our Lord Jesus Christ—Christ bought us with His blood and made us free from the Law.

God has shown His love to us by sending His only Son into the world. . .so we might have life through Christ. This is love! It is not that we loved God but that He loved us. For God sent His Son to pay for our sins with His own blood—God makes anyone right with Himself who puts his trust in Jesus.

Ps. 90:11; Matt. 27:45–46—Isa. 53:6; Rom. 8:1— Rom. 5:1—Gal. 3:13; 1 John 4:9–10—Rom. 3:26.

You do not get things because you do not ask for them.

Ask, and what you are asking for will be given to you. Look, and. . .you will find. Knock, and the door you are knocking on will be opened to you. Everyone who asks receives what he asks for. Everyone who looks finds what he is looking for. Everyone who knocks has the door opened to him—We are sure that if we ask anything that He wants us to have, He will hear us. If we are sure He hears us when we ask, we can be sure He will give us what we ask for—If you do not have wisdom, ask God for it. He is always ready to give it to you and will never say you are wrong for asking—Open your mouth wide and I will fill it—Men should always pray and not give up.

The eyes of the Lord are on those who do what is right and good. His ears are open to their cry. . . . He hears them. And He takes them from all their troubles—You will ask in My name. I will not ask the Father for you because the Father loves you. . .because you love Me. . . . Ask and you will receive. Then your joy will be full.

Ezek. 36:37; James 4:2; Matt. 7:7–8—1 John 5:14–15—James 1:5—Ps. 81:10—Luke 18:1; Ps. 34:15, 17—John 16:26–27, 24.

O Lord, I know that what You decide is right and good. You punish me because You are faithful—O Lord, You are our Father. We are the clay, and You are our pot maker. All of us are the work of Your hand—It is the Lord. Let Him do what is good in His eyes.

You are right and good, O Lord, when I complain to You about my trouble. Yet I would like to talk with You about what is fair.

He will sit as one who melts silver and makes it pure—The Lord punishes everyone He loves. He whips every son He receives—A follower should be happy to be as his teacher, and a servant who is owned by someone should be happy to be as his owner—He learned to obey by the things He suffered.

Be happy that you are able to share some of the suffering of Christ. When His shining-greatness is shown, you will be filled with much joy—These are the ones who came out of the time of much trouble. They have washed their clothes and have made them white in the blood of the Lamb.

JOB 2:10; PS. 119:75—ISA. 64:8—1 SAM. 3:18; JER. 12:1; MAL. 3:3—HEB. 12:6—MATT. 10:25—HEB. 5:8; 1 PET. 4:13—REV. 7:14.

When the one who hates us comes in like a flood, the Spirit of the Lord will lift up a wall against him.—Get away, Satan. It is written, You must worship the Lord your God. You must obey Him only. Then the devil went away from Jesus. Angels came and cared for Him.

Be strong with the Lord's strength. Put on the things God gives you to fight with. Then you will not fall into the traps of the devil.—Have nothing to do with the bad things done in darkness. Instead, show that these things are wrong.—Keep awake! Watch at all times. The devil is working against you. He is walking around like a hungry lion with his mouth open. He is looking for someone to eat.—The way we have power over the sins of the world is by our faith.

Who can say anything against the people God has chosen? It is God Who says they are right with Himself.

JAMES 4:7; ISA. 59:19—MATT. 4:10–11; EPH. 6:10–11—EPH. 5:11—PET. 5:8—1 JOHN 5:4; ROM. 8:33.

Who among you fears the Lord and obeys the voice of His Servant, yet walks in darkness and has no light? Let him trust in the name of the Lord and have faith in his God.

You will look for Me and find Me, when you look for Me with all your heart—Look, and what you are looking for you will find. Knock, and the door you are knocking on will be opened to you. For everyone who asks, will receive what he asks for. Everyone who looks, will find what he is looking for. Everyone who knocks, will have the door opened to him.

Share together with us what we have with the Father and with His Son, Jesus Christ—At one time you were far away from God. Now you have been brought close to Him. Christ did this for you when He gave His blood on the cross. Now all of us can go to the Father through Christ by way of the one Holy Spirit.

If we say we are joined together with Him but live in darkness, we are telling a lie. We are not living the truth.

I am with you always—I will never leave you or let you be alone—[The] Helper. . .will be with you forever.

JOB 23:3; ISA. 50:10; JER. 29:13—LUKE 11:9–10; 1 JOHN 1:3—EPH. 2:13, 18; 1 JOHN 1:6; MATT. 28:20—HEB. 13:5—JOHN 14:16–17.

Test me and try me, O Lord. Test my mind and my heart—See, You want truth deep within the heart. And You will make me know wisdom in the hidden part—I thought about my ways and turned my steps to Your Law. I hurried and did not wait to obey Your Law—A man should look into his own heart and life before eating the bread and drinking from the cup.

If we tell Him our sins, He is faithful and we can depend on Him to forgive us of our sins. He will make our lives clean from all sin—There is One Who will go between him and the Father. . .Jesus Christ, the One Who is right with God. He paid for our sins with His own blood—Christian brothers, now we know we can go into the Holiest Place of All because the blood of Jesus was given. . .by the new and living way. Christ made this way for us. He opened the curtain, which was His own body. We have a great Religious Leader over the house of God. . . . Let us come near to God with a true heart full of faith. Our hearts must be made clean from guilty feelings and our bodies washed with pure water.

LAM. 3:40; PS. 26:2—PS. 51:6—PS. 119:59–60—1 COR. 11:28; 1 JOHN 1:9—1 JOHN 2:1–2—HEB. 10:19–22.

This is something special to see for all time, because of the agreement that I am making between Me and you and every living thing that is with you: I will set My rainbow in the cloud, and. . .I will look upon it to remember the agreement that will last forever between God and every living thing of all flesh that is on the earth—An agreement with me that lasts forever. It is planned right in all things, and sure—God gave these two things that cannot be changed and God cannot lie. We who have turned to Him can have great comfort knowing that He will do what He has promised.

We bring you the Good News about the promise made to our early fathers. God has finished this for us who are their children. He did this by raising Jesus from the dead.

Jesus Christ is the same yesterday and today and forever.

REV. 4:3; GEN. 9:12–13, 16—2 SAM. 23:5—HEB. 6:18; ACTS 13:32–33; HEB. 13:8.

Think of yourselves as dead to the power of sin.
But now you have new life because
of Jesus Christ our Lord.

Anyone who hears My Word and puts his trust in Him
Who sent Me has life that lasts forever. He will not be
guilty. He has already passed from death into life—The
Law has no power over me. I am dead to the Law. Now
I can live for God. I have been put up on the cross to die
with Christ. I no longer live. Christ lives in me. The life I
now live in this body, I live by putting my trust in the Son
of God. He was the One Who loved me and gave Himself
for me.

Because I live, you will live also—I give them life
that lasts forever. They will never be punished. No one
is able to take them out of My hand. My Father Who
gave them to Me is greater than all. No one is able to
take them out of My Father's hand. My Father and I
are one!

If then you have been raised with Christ, keep looking for the good things of heaven. . .where Christ is
seated on the right side of God. You are dead to the
things of this world. Your new life is now hidden in
God through Christ.

ROM. 6:11; JOHN 5:24—GAL. 2:19–20; JOHN 14:19—
JOHN 10:28–30; COL. 3:1, 3.

Woman, where are those who spoke against you? Has no man said you are guilty? She said, No one, Sir. Jesus said to her, Neither do I say you are guilty. Go on your way and do not sin again.

The loving-favor of God came to many people also. This gift came also by one Man Jesus Christ, God's Son . . . . The free gift makes men right with God.

God had so much loving-kindness. He loved us with such a great love. Even when we were dead because of our sins, He made us alive by what Christ did for us. You have been saved from the punishment of sin by His loving-favor. God raised us up from death when He raised up Christ Jesus. He has given us a place with Christ in the heavens. He did this to show us through all the time to come the great riches of His loving-favor. He has shown us His kindness through Christ Jesus.

God did not keep His own Son for Himself but gave Him for us all. Then with His Son, will He not give us all things?

JAMES 1:5; JOHN 8:10–11; ROM. 5:15–16; EPH. 2:4–7; ROM. 8:32

For God so loved the world that He gave
His only Son. Whoever puts his trust in God's
Son will not be lost but will have life
that lasts forever.

God. . .is the One Who brought us to Himself when we hated Him. . .through Christ. Then He gave us the work of bringing others to Him. God was in Christ. He was working through Christ to bring the whole world back to Himself. God no longer held men's sins against them. And He gave us the work of telling and showing men this. We are Christ's missionaries. . .speaking for Christ and we ask you from our hearts to turn from your sins and come to God. Christ never sinned but God put our sin on Him. Then we are made right with God because of what Christ has done for us—God is love. God has shown His love to us by sending His only Son into the world. . .so we might have life through Christ. This is love! It is not that we loved God but that He loved us. For God sent His Son to pay for our sins with His own blood. Dear friends, if God loved us that much, then we should love each other.

JOHN 3:16; 2 COR. 5:18–21—1 JOHN 4:8–11.

Anyone of you who is without sin can throw the first stone at her. When they heard what He said, they went away one by one, beginning with the older ones until they were all gone.

Who told you that you were without clothes? Have you eaten from the tree of which I told you not to eat?

If you know what is right to do but you do not do it, you sin—Our heart may say that we have done wrong...God is greater than our heart. He knows everything. Dear friends, if our heart does not say that we are wrong, we will have no fear as we stand before Him.

All...is good.... But it is wrong to eat anything that will make someone fall into sin.... A man is happy if he knows he is doing right.

Look into me, O God, and know my heart. Try me and know my thoughts. See if there is any sinful way in me and lead me in the way that lasts forever.

Prov. 20:27; John 8:7, 9; Gen. 3:11; James 4:17—1 John 3:20–21; Rom. 14:20, 22; Ps. 139:23–24.

Now is the right time! See! Now is the day to be saved—The Light will be with you for a little while yet. Go on your way while you have the Light so you will not be in the dark. When a man is walking in the dark, he does not know where he is going. While you have the Light, put your trust in the Light. Then you will be the sons of the Light.

Whatever your hand finds to do, do it with all your strength. For there is no work or planning or learning or wisdom in the place of the dead where you are going.

Soul, you have many good things put away in your building. . .for many years to come. Now rest and eat and drink and have lots of fun. . . . You fool! Tonight your soul will be taken from you. Then who will have all the things you have put away? It is the same with a man who puts away riches for himself and does not have the riches of God.

What is your life? It is like fog. You see it and soon it is gone—The world and all its desires will pass away. But the man who obeys God and does what He wants done will live forever.

PROV. 27:1; 2 COR. 6:2—JOHN 12:35–36; ECCLES. 9:10; LUKE 12:19–21; JAMES 4:14—1 JOHN 2:17.

Before the mountains were born, before You gave birth to the earth and the world, forever and ever, You are God.

I, the Lord, do not change. So you, O children of Jacob, are not destroyed—Jesus Christ is the same yesterday and today and forever.

Whatever is good and perfect comes to us from God. He is the One Who made all light. He does not change. No shadow is made by His turning—God does not change His mind when He chooses men and gives them His gifts.

God is not a man, that He should lie. He is not a son of man, that He should be sorry for what He has said—It is because of the Lord's loving-kindness that we are not destroyed for His loving-pity never ends.

But Jesus lives forever. He is the Religious Leader forever. It will never change. And so Jesus is able, now and forever, to save from the punishment of sin all who come to God through Him because He lives forever to pray for them—Do not be afraid. I am the First and the Last.

Ps. 102:27; Ps. 90:2; Mal. 3:6—Heb. 13:8; James 1:17—Rom. 11:29; Num. 23:19—Lam. 3:22; Heb. 7:24–25—Rev. 1:17.

God is love. If you live in love, you live by the help of
God and God lives in you—The love of God has come
into our hearts through the Holy Spirit Who was
given to us—This Stone is of great worth to you who have
your trust in Him—We love Him because He loved us
first—For the love of Christ puts us into action. We are
sure that Christ died for everyone. So, because of that,
everyone has a part in His death. Christ died for everyone
so that they would live for Him. They should not live to
please themselves but for Christ Who died on a cross and
was raised from the dead for them.

God has taught you to love each other—This is
what I tell you to do: Love each other just as I have
loved you—Most of all, have a true love for each other.
Love covers many sins—Live with love as Christ loved
you. He gave Himself for us, a gift on the altar to God
which was as a sweet smell to God.

GAL 5:22; 1 JOHN 4:16—ROM. 5:5—1 PET. 2:7—1 JOHN
4:19—2 COR. 5:14–15; 1 THESS. 4:9—JOHN 15:12—1
PET. 4:8—EPH. 5:2.

Since God is for us, who can be against us?—The Lord is with me. I will not be afraid of what man can do to me.

You have given a flag to those who fear You.

The Lord is my light and the One Who saves me. Whom should I fear? The Lord is the strength of my life. Of whom should I be afraid? Even if an army gathers against me, my heart will not be afraid. Even if war rises against me, I will be sure of You.

Now see, God is with us at our head—The Lord of All is with us. The God of Jacob is our strong place.

These kings will fight and make war with the Lamb. But the Lamb will win the war. Why are the nations so shaken up and the people planning foolish things? He Who sits in the heavens laughs. The Lord makes fun of them—Make a plan, but it will come to nothing. Give your plan, but it will not be done. For God is with us.

EXOD. 17:15; ROM. 8:31—PS. 118:6; PS. 60:4; PS. 27:1, 3; 2 CHRON. 13:12—PS. 46:7; REV. 17:14; PS. 2:1, 4—ISA. 8:10.

We give thanks to the God and Father of our Lord Jesus Christ. He is our Father Who shows us lovingkindness and our God Who gives us comfort. He gives us comfort in all our troubles. Then we can comfort other people who have the same troubles. We give the same kind of comfort God gives us. As we have suffered much for Christ and have shared in His pain, we also share His great comfort.

With this hope you can be happy even if you need to have sorrow and all kinds of tests for awhile. These tests have come to prove your faith and to show that it is good. Gold, which can be destroyed, is tested by fire. Your faith is worth much more than gold and it must be tested also. Then your faith will bring thanks and shining-greatness and honor to Jesus Christ when He comes again—But the Lord was with me.

So if God wants you to suffer, give yourself to Him. He will do what is right for you. He made you and He is faithful.

GEN. 41:52; 2 COR. 1:3–5; 1 PET. 1:6–7—2 TIM. 4:17; 1 PET. 4:19.

There the troubles of the sinful stop. There the tired are at rest. Those in prison are at rest together. They do not hear the voice of the one who rules over their work.

Those who are dead who died belonging to the Lord will be happy. . . . They will have rest from all their work. All the good things they have done will follow them.

Our friend Lazarus is sleeping. . . . But Jesus meant Lazarus was dead. They thought He meant Lazarus was resting in sleep.

While we are in this body, we cry inside ourselves because things are hard for us—We also cry inside ourselves, even we who have received the Holy Spirit. . .the first of God's gifts to us. We are waiting to become His complete sons when our bodies are made free. We were saved with this hope ahead of us. Now hope means we are waiting for something we do not have. How can a man hope for something he already has? But if we hope for something we do not yet see, we must learn how to wait for it.

HEB. 4:9; JOB 3:17–18; REV. 14:13; JOHN 11:11, 13; 2 COR. 5:4—ROM. 8:23–25.

> *Trust in the Lord with all your heart, and do not trust in your own understanding. Agree with Him in all your ways, and He will make your paths straight.*

Trust in Him at all times, O people. Pour out your heart before Him. God is a safe place for us—I will show you and teach you in the way you should go. I will tell you what to do with My eye upon you. Do not be like the horse or the donkey which have no understanding. They must be made to work by using bits and leather ropes or they will not come to you. Many are the sorrows of the sinful. But loving-kindness will be all around the man who trusts in the Lord—Your ears will hear a word behind you, saying, This is the way, walk in it, whenever you turn to the right or to the left.

If You Yourself do not go with us, do not have us leave this place. For how will it be known that I and Your people have found favor in Your eyes, unless You go with us? Then I and Your people will be different from all the other people on the earth.

PROV. 3:5–6; PS. 62:8—PS. 32:8–10—ISA. 30:21; EXOD. 33:15–16.

Y ou will have riches in heaven. Come and follow Me—I am. . .your [very great] reward.

You have done well. You are a good and faithful servant. You have been faithful over a few things. I will put many things in your care. Come and share my joy—They will be leaders forever.

You will get the crown of shining-greatness that will not come to an end—The crown of life—A crown which comes from being right with God—A prize that will last forever.

Father, I want My followers You gave Me to be with Me where I am. Then they may see My shining-greatness which You gave Me—We will. . .be with Him forever.

I am sure that our suffering now cannot be compared to the shining-greatness that He is going to give us.

PHIL. 3:14; MATT. 19:21—GEN. 15:1; MATT. 25:21—REV. 22:5; 1 PET. 5:4—JAMES 1:12—2 TIM. 4:8—1 COR. 9:25; JOHN 17:24—1 THESS. 4:17; ROM. 8:18.

Keep your minds thinking about things in heaven.
Do not think about things on the earth.

Do not love the world or anything in the world. If anyone loves the world, the Father's love is not in him—Do not gather together for yourself riches of this earth. They will be eaten by bugs and become rusted. Men can break in and steal them. Gather together riches in heaven where they will not be eaten by bugs or become rusted. Men cannot break in and steal them. For wherever your riches are, your heart will be there also.

Our life is lived by faith. . .not. . .by what we see in front of us—This is the reason we do not give up. Our human body is wearing out. But our spirits are getting stronger every day. The little troubles we suffer now for a short time are making us ready for the great things God is going to give us forever. We do not look at the things that can be seen. We look at the things that cannot be seen. The things that can be seen will come to an end. But the things that cannot be seen will last forever—The great things. . .we have been promised. . .are being kept safe in heaven for us. They are pure and will not pass away.

COL. 3:2; 1 JOHN 2:15—MATT. 6:19–21; 2 COR. 5:7—2 COR. 4:16–18—1 PET. 1:4.

See how the early preachers spoke for the Lord by their suffering and by being willing to wait—All these things happened to show us something. They were written to teach us that the end of the world is near.

Should we receive good from God and not receive trouble? In all this Job did not sin with his lips—Aaron said nothing—It is the Lord. Let Him do what is good in His eyes—Give all your cares to the Lord and He will give you strength—For sure He took on Himself our troubles and carried our sorrows.

Come to Me, all of you who work and have heavy loads. I will give you rest. Follow My teachings and learn from Me. I am gentle and do not have pride. You will have rest for your souls. For My way of carrying a load is easy and My load is not heavy.

GEN. 49:15; JAMES 5:10—1 COR. 10:11; JOB 2:10—LEV. 10:3—1 SAM. 3:18—PS. 55:22—ISA. 53:4; MATT. 11:28–30.

I lift up my eyes to You, O You Whose throne is in the heavens. See, the eyes of servants look to the hand of their owner. The eyes of a woman servant look to the hand of her owner. So our eyes look to the Lord our God, until He shows us loving-kindness—Hear my cry, O God. Listen to my prayer. I call to You from the end of the earth when my heart is weak. Lead me to the rock that is higher than I. For You have been a safe place for me, a tower of strength where I am safe from those who fight against me. Let me live in Your tent forever. Let me be safe under the covering of Your wings—For You have been a strong-place for those who could not help themselves and for those in need because of much trouble. You have been a safe place from the storm.

Christ suffered for us. This shows us we are to follow in His steps. He never sinned. No lie or bad talk ever came from His lips. When people spoke against Him, He never spoke back. When He suffered from what people did to Him, He did not try to pay them back. He left it in the hands of the One Who is always right in judging.

Isa. 38:14; Ps. 123:1–2—Ps. 61:1–4—Isa. 25:4; 1 Pet. 2:21–23.

We had all kinds of trouble. There was fighting all around us. Our hearts were afraid—Do not be afraid. For those who are with us are more than those who are with them—Be strong with the Lord's strength.

You come to me with a sword and spears. But I come to you in the name of the Lord of All, the God of the armies of Israel, Whom you have stood against—God is my strong place. . . . He makes my hands ready for battle, so that my arms can use a bow of brass—God makes us able to do these things.

The angel of the Lord stays close around those who fear Him, and He takes them out of trouble—The mountain was full of horses and war-wagons of fire all around Elisha.

There is not enough time to tell of [those who] had faith that they won wars over other countries. . . . They were made strong again after they had been weak and sick. They were strong in war. They made fighting men from other countries run home.

1 Tim 6:12; 2 Cor 7:5—2 Kings 6:16—Eph 6:10; 1 Sam 17:45—2 Sam 22:33, 35—2 Cor 3:5; Ps 34:7—2 Kings 6:17; Heb 11:32–34.

The Lord your God. . .goes before you on your way. He finds a place for you to set up your tents. He uses fire to show you the way to go during the night. During the day He uses a cloud to lead you.—Like an eagle that shakes its nest, that flies over its young, He spread His wings and caught them. He carried them on His wings. The Lord alone led him.—The steps of a good man are led by the Lord. And He is happy in his way. When he falls, he will not be thrown down, because the Lord holds his hand.—A man who does what is right and good may have many troubles. But the Lord takes him out of them all.—For the Lord knows the way of those who are right with Him. But the way of the sinful will be lost from God forever.—We know that God makes all things work together for the good of those who love Him and are chosen to be a part of His plan.—We have the Lord our God with us, to help us and to fight our battles.

The Lord your God is with you, a Powerful One Who wins the battle. He will have much joy over you.

PROV. 2:8; DEUT. 1:32–33—DEUT. 32:11–12—PS. 37:23–24—PS. 34:19—PS. 1:6—ROM. 8:28—2 CHRON. 32:8; ZEPH. 3:17.

But He was hurt for our wrongdoing. He was crushed for our sins. He was punished so we would have peace . . .The Lord has put on Him the sin of us all. . .He was hurt because of the sin of the people who should have been punished. But it was the will of the Lord to crush Him, causing Him to suffer.

Jesus our Lord. . .died for our sins—Christ suffered and died for sins once for all. He never sinned and yet He died for us who have sinned. He died so He might bring us to God—He carried our sins in His own body when He died on a cross. In doing this, we may be dead to sin and alive to all that is right and good. His wounds have healed you!

Christ never sinned but God put our sin on Him. Then we are made right with God because of what Christ has done for us.

Christ bought us with His blood and made us free from the Law. . . . Christ did this by carrying the load and by being punished instead of us.

MATT. 27:46; ISA. 53:5–6, 8, 10; ROM. 4:24–25—1 PET. 3:18—1 PET. 2:24; 2 COR. 5:21; GAL. 3:13.

This is hard to understand, but it shows that the church is the body of Christ.

You will no longer be called Left Alone.... But you will be called My joy is in her.... For the Lord finds joy in you.... And as the man to be married finds joy in his bride, so your God will find joy in you—The Lord has chosen me...to comfort all who are filled with sorrow. To those who have sorrow in Zion I will give them a crown of beauty instead of ashes. I will give them the oil of joy instead of sorrow, and a spirit of praise instead of a spirit of no hope.

I will have much joy in the Lord. My soul will have joy in my God, for He has clothed me with the clothes of His saving power...as a man at his own wedding wears something special on his head, and as a bride makes herself beautiful with stones of great worth.

I will promise to make you Mine forever. Yes, I will take you as My bride in what is right and good and fair, and in loving-kindness and in loving-pity.

Who can keep us away from the love of Christ?

Isa. 54:5; Eph. 5:32; Isa. 62:4–5—Isa. 61:1–3; Isa. 61:10; Hos. 2:19; Rom. 8:35.

All Your holy ones are in Your hand—The word of the Lord came to [Elijah], saying, Leave here and turn east. Hide yourself by the river Cherith, east of the Jordan. You will drink from the river. And I have told the ravens to bring food to you there. Then the word of the Lord came to him, saying, Get up and go to Zarephath, which belongs to Sidon, and stay there. I have told a woman there, whose husband has died, to feed you.

Do not worry about your life. Do not worry about what you are going to eat and drink. Do not worry about what you are going to wear. . . . Your Father in heaven knows you need all these things.

Trust in the Lord with all your heart, and do not trust in your own understanding. Agree with Him in all your ways, and He will make your paths straight—Give all your worries to Him because He cares for you.

Ps. 31:15; Deut. 33:3—1 Kings 17:2–4, 8–9; Matt. 6:25, 32; Prov. 3:5–6—1 Pet. 5:7.

Who is a God like You, Who forgives sin and the wrong-doing of Your chosen people who are left? He does not stay angry forever because He is happy to show lovingkindness. He will again have loving-pity on us. He will crush our sins under foot. Yes, You will throw all our sins into the deep sea.

For a short time I left you, but with much loving-pity I will take you back. When I was very angry I hid My face from you for a short time. But with loving-kindness that lasts forever I will have pity on you, says the Lord Who bought you and saves you—I will forgive their sins. I will remember their sins no more.

How happy he is whose wrongdoing is forgiven, and whose sin is covered! How happy is the man whose sin the Lord does not hold against him, and in whose spirit there is nothing false—The blood of Jesus Christ, His Son, makes our lives clean from all sin.

Isa. 38:17; Mic. 7:18–19; Isa. 54:7–8—Jer. 31:34; Ps. 32:1–2—1 John 1:7.

Able to do much more than we ask or think. . .
[Able to] give you all you need. . .more than enough
. . .everything you need for yourselves. . .enough left over
to give when there is a need.

Able to help us when we are tempted.

Able. . .to save from the punishment of sin all who
come to God through Him because He lives forever to
pray for them.

[Able to] keep you from falling and can bring you before Himself free from all sin. He can give you great joy.

Able to keep safe that which I have trusted to Him
until the day He comes again.

He will change these bodies of ours of the earth
and make them. . .like His body of shining-greatness.
He has the power to do this because He can make all
things obey Him.

Do you have faith that I can do this? . . . Yes, Sir! . . .
You will have what you want because you have faith.

2 Tim. 1:12; Eph. 3:20; 2 Cor. 9:8; Heb. 2:18; Heb.
7:25; Jude 24; 2 Tim. 1:12; Phil. 3:21; Matt. 9:28–29.

Be careful not to forget the Lord your God by not keeping all His Laws which I am telling you today. When you have eaten and are filled, and have built good houses to live in. . .be careful not to become proud. Do not forget the Lord your God. . . . For it is He Who is giving you power to become rich.

Unless the Lord builds the house, its builders work for nothing. Unless the Lord watches over the city, the men who watch over it stay awake for nothing. You rise up early, and go to bed late, and work hard for your food, all for nothing. For the Lord gives to His loved ones even while they sleep—It was not by their sword that they took the land. Their own arm did not save them. But it was Your right hand, and Your arm, and the light of Your face, for You favored them—Many are asking, Who will show us any good? Let the light of Your face shine on us, O Lord.

1 Tim. 6:17; Deut. 8:11–12, 14, 18; Ps. 127:1–2—Ps. 44:3—Ps. 4:6.

The new and living way. . . Christ made this way for us—Not because we worked to be right with God. It was because of His loving-kindness that He washed our sins away. At the same time He gave us new life when the Holy Spirit came into our lives. . .to fill our lives through Jesus Christ, the One Who saves—For by His loving-favor you have been saved from the punishment of sin through faith. It is not by anything you have done. It is a gift of God. It is not given to you because you worked for it. If you could work for it, you would be proud.

Let honor be given to Your name and not to us, O Lord, not to us—The One Who loves us and has set us free from our sins by His blood. . .has made us a holy nation of religious leaders who can go to His God and Father. He is the One to receive honor and power forever! Let it be so—You were killed. Your blood has bought men for God from every family and from every language and from every kind of people and from every nation—I saw many people. No one could tell how many there were. . . . They were crying out with a loud voice, We are saved from the punishment of sin by our God Who sits on the throne and by the Lamb!

REV. 14:3; HEB. 10:20—TITUS. 3:5–6—EPH. 2:8–9; PS. 115:1—REV. 1:5–6:—REV. 5:9—REV. 7:9–10.

God will have for Himself a lamb ready for the burnt gift.

See, the Lord's hand is not so short that it cannot save, and His ear is not closed that it cannot hear—The One Who saves from the punishment of sin will come out of Jerusalem. He will turn the Jews from doing sinful things.

Happy is he whose help is the God of Jacob, and whose hope is in the Lord his God—See, the eye of the Lord is on those who fear Him, and on those who hope for His loving-kindness, to save their soul from death.

And my God will give you everything you need because of His great riches in Christ Jesus—God has said, I will never leave you or let you be alone. So we can say for sure, The Lord is my Helper. I am not afraid of anything man can do to me—The Lord is my strength and my safe cover. My heart trusts in Him, and I am helped. So my heart is full of joy. I will thank Him with my song.

GEN. 22:14; GEN. 22:8; ISA. 59:1—ROM. 11:26; PS 146:5—PS. 33:18–19; PHIL. 4:19—HEB. 13:5–6—PS. 28:7.

Where two or three are gathered together in My name, there I am with them—The one who loves Me will obey My teaching. My Father will love him. We will come to him and live with him.

If you obey My teaching, you will live in My love. In this way, I have obeyed My Father's teaching and live in His love.

May my loved one come into his garden and eat its best fruits—I have come into my garden, my sister, my bride. I have gathered my perfume with my spice. I have eaten my honey and the comb—But the fruit that comes from having the Holy Spirit in our lives is: love, joy, peace, not giving up, being kind, being good, having faith, being gentle, and being the boss over our own desires.

When you give much fruit, My Father is honored. This shows you are My followers—Any branch that gives fruit, He cuts it back so it will give more fruit— Be filled with the fruits of right living. These come from Jesus Christ, with honor and thanks to God.

SONG OF SOL. 2:16; MATT. 18:20—JOHN 14:23; JOHN 15:10; SONG OF SOL. 4:16–5:1—GAL. 5:22–23; JOHN 15:8—JOHN 15:2—PHIL. 1:11.

The good that comes from the Lord makes one rich, and He adds no sorrow to it—For You will make those happy who do what is right, O Lord. You will cover them all around with Your favor.

He will not let your feet go out from under you. He Who watches over you will not sleep. Listen, He Who watches over Israel will not close his eyes or sleep. The Lord watches over you. The Lord is your safe cover at your right hand. The Lord will keep you from all that is sinful. He will watch over your soul. The Lord will watch over your coming and going, now and forever—I, the Lord, am its keeper. I water it all the time. I watch over it day and night.

Holy Father, keep those You have given to Me in the power of Your name. . . . While I have been with them in the world, I have kept them in the power of Your name. I have kept watch over those You gave Me.

The Lord will look after me and will keep me from every sinful plan they have. He will bring me safe into His holy nation of heaven. May He have all the shining-greatness forever. Let it be so.

Num. 6:24; Prov. 10:22—Ps. 5:12; Ps. 121:3–5, 7–8—Isa. 27:3; John 17:11–12; 2 Tim. 4:18.

A man of sorrows and suffering, knowing sadness well—Our Religious Leader understands how weak we are—God made all things. He made all things for Himself. It was right for God to make Jesus a perfect Leader by having Him suffer for men's sins. In this way, He is bringing many men to share His shining-greatness— Even being God's Son, He learned to obey by the things He suffered.

I obeyed Him. I did not turn back. I gave My back to those who hit Me, and My face to those who pull out the hair on my face. I did not cover My face from shame and spit.

See how much He loved—Jesus did not come to help angels. Instead, He came to help men who are of Abraham's family. So Jesus had to become like His brothers in every way. He had to be one of us to be our Religious Leader to go between God and us. He had loving-pity on us and He was faithful. He gave Himself as a gift to die on a cross for our sins so that God would not hold these sins against us any longer.

JOHN 11:35; ISA. 53:3—HEB. 4:15—HEB. 2:10—HEB. 5:8; ISA. 50:5–6; JOHN 11:36—HEB. 2:16–17.

*May the Lord make His face shine upon you,
and be kind to you. May the Lord show favor
toward you, and give you peace.*

No man has ever seen God. But Christ has made God known to us—The Son shines with the shining-greatness of the Father. The Son is as God is in every way—The eyes of those who do not believe are made blind by Satan who is the god of this world. He does not want the light of the Good News to shine in their hearts. This Good News shines as the shining-greatness of Christ. Christ is as God is.

Make Your face shine upon your servant. Save me in Your loving-kindness. Do not let me be put to shame, O Lord. For I call to You—O Lord, by Your favor You have made my mountain stand strong. But when You hid Your face, I was troubled—How happy are the people who know the sound of joy! They walk in the light of Your face, O Lord.

The Lord will give strength to His people. The Lord will give His people peace—Take hope. It is I. Do not be afraid!

Num. 6:25–26; John 1:18—Heb. 1:3—2 Cor. 4:4; Ps. 31:16–17—Ps. 30:7—Ps. 89:15; Ps. 29:11—Matt. 14:27.

A man cannot please God unless he has faith—Those who do what their sinful old selves want to do cannot please God—For the Lord is happy with His people.

This shows you have received loving-favor when you are even punished for doing what is right because of your trust in God. . . . If you are beaten when you have done what is right, and do not try to get out of it, God is pleased—Your beauty should be a gentle and quiet spirit. In God's sight this is of great worth.

He who gives a gift of thanks honors Me. And to him who makes his way right, I will show him the saving power of God—I will praise the name of God with song. And I will give Him great honor with much thanks. This will please the Lord more than any ox or young bull with horns and hoofs.

Christian brothers, I ask you from my heart to give your bodies to God because of His loving-kindness to us. . .a living and holy gift given to God. . . . This is the true worship that you should give Him.

1 John 3:22; Heb. 11:6—Rom. 8:8—Ps. 149:4; 1 Pet. 2:19–20—1 Pet. 3:4; Ps. 50:23—Ps. 69:30–31; Rom. 12:1.

It is true that we share the same kind of flesh and blood because Jesus became a man like us. He died as we must die.

Look to Me and be saved, all the ends of the earth. For I am God, and there is no other.

There is One Who will go between him and the Father. He is Jesus Christ, the One Who is right with God—At one time you were far away from God. Now you have been brought close to Him. Christ did this for you when He gave His blood on the cross. We have peace because of Christ—Christ went into the Holiest Place of All one time for all people. . . . He gave His own blood. By doing this, He bought us with His own blood and made us free from sin forever. Christ is the One Who gave us this New Way of Worship. All those who have been called by God may receive life that lasts forever just as He promised them—And so Jesus is able, now and forever, to save from the punishment of sin all who come to God through Him because He lives forever to pray for them.

1 Tim. 2:5; Heb. 2:14; Isa. 45:22; 1 John 2:1—Eph. 2:13–14—Heb. 9:12, 15—Heb. 7:25.

Y ou will keep the man in perfect peace whose mind is kept on You, because he trusts in You. Trust in the Lord forever. For the Lord God is a Rock that lasts forever.

Give all your cares to the Lord and He will give you strength—He has not turned away from the suffering of the one in pain or trouble. He has not hidden His face from him. But He has heard his cry for help—Is anyone among you suffering? He should pray.

Do not let your hearts be troubled or afraid—Do not worry about your life. Do not worry about what you are going to eat and drink. Do not worry about what you are going to wear. . . . Look at the birds in the sky. They do not plant seeds. They do not gather grain. They do not put grain into a building to keep. Yet your Father in heaven feeds them! Are you not more important than the birds?—Do not doubt, believe!—I am with you always!

Ps. 42:6; Isa. 26:3–4; Ps. 55:22—Ps. 22:24—James 5:13; John 14:27—Matt. 6:25–26—John 20:27—Matt. 28:20.

Live your lives as the Good News of Christ says you should—Keep away from everything that even looks like sin—If men speak bad of you because you are a Christian, you will be happy. . . . None of you should suffer as one who kills another person or as one who steals or as one who makes trouble or as one who tries to be the boss of other peoples' lives—Be without blame. You are God's children and no one can talk against you, even in a sin-loving and sin-sick world. You are to shine as lights among the sinful people of this world—Let your light shine in front of men. Then they will see the good things you do and will honor your Father Who is in heaven.

Do not let kindness and truth leave you. Tie them around your neck. Write them upon your heart. So you will find favor and good understanding in the eyes of God and man—Christian brothers, keep your minds thinking about whatever is true, whatever is respected, whatever is right, whatever is pure, whatever can be loved, and whatever is well thought of. If there is anything good and worth giving thanks for, think about these things.

TITUS 2:10; PHIL. 1:27—1 THESS. 5:22—1 PET. 4:14–15—PHIL. 2:15—MATT. 5:16; PROV. 3:3–4—PHIL. 4:8.

He gave us our new lives through the truth of His Word only because He wanted to.—The Law brings death, but the Holy Spirit gives life. Christ loved the church. He gave His life for it. Christ did this so He could set the church apart for Himself. He made it clean by the washing of water with the Word. Christ did this so the church might stand before Him in shining-greatness. There is to be no sin of any kind in it.

How can a young man keep his way pure? By living by Your Word. Your Word has given me new life. Your Word have I hid in my heart, that I may not sin against You. I will be glad in Your Law. I will not forget Your Word. . . . I trust in Your Word. The Law of Your mouth is better to me than thousands of gold and silver pieces. I will never forget Your Word for by it You have given me new life. How sweet is Your Word to my taste! It is sweeter than honey to my mouth! I get understanding from Your Law and so I hate every false way.

Jt. 6:63; James 1:18—2 Cor. 3:6; Eph. 5:25–27; Ps. 119:9, 50, 11, 16, 42, 72, 93, 103–104.

My soul is very sad. My soul is so full of sorrow I am ready to die. You stay here and watch with Me. He went on a little farther and got down with His face on the ground. He prayed, My Father, if it can be done, take away what is before Me. Even so, not what I want but what You want—His heart was much troubled and He prayed all the more. Water ran from His face like blood and fell to the ground.

The strings of death are all around me. And the fear of the grave came upon me. I suffered with trouble and sorrow—Being put to shame has broken my heart, and I feel very sick. I looked for pity but there was none. I looked for someone to comfort me but there was no one—Look to the right and see. For there is no one who thinks about me. There is no place for me to go to be safe. No one cares about my soul.

He was hated and men would have nothing to do with Him, a man of sorrows and suffering, knowing sadness well. We hid, as it were, our faces from Him. He was hated, and we did not think well of Him.

HEB. 2:10; MATT. 26:38–39—LUKE 22:44; PS. 116:3— PS. 69:20—PS. 142:4; ISA. 53:3.

The heavens are telling of the greatness of God and the great open spaces above show the work of His hands— The heavens were made by the Word of the Lord. All the stars were made by the breath of His mouth. For He spoke, and it was done. He spoke with strong words, and it stood strong—See, the nations are like a drop in a pail. Their weight is like a little piece of dust. See, He lifts up the islands like fine dust.

Through faith we understand that the world was made by the Word of God. Things we see were made from what could not be seen.

When I look up and think about Your heavens, the work of Your fingers, the moon and the stars, which You have set in their place, what is man, that You think of him, the son of man that You care for him?

EXOD. 20:11; Ps. 19:1—Ps. 33:6, 9—ISA. 40:15; HEB. 11:3; Ps. 8:3–4.

My days go faster than a runner. They fly away, and see no good. They go by like fast boats, like an eagle coming down to catch its food—You carry men away as with a flood. They fall asleep. In the morning they are like the new grass that grows. It grows well in the morning, but dries up and dies by evening—Man who is born of woman lives only a short time and is full of trouble. He grows up and dries like a flower.

The world and all its desires will pass away. But the man who obeys God and does what He wants done will live forever—They will be destroyed but You will always live. They will all become old as clothing becomes old. You will change them like a coat. And they will be changed, but You are always the same. Your years will never end—Jesus Christ is the same yesterday and today and forever.

JAMES 4:14; JOB 9:25–26—Ps. 90:5–6—JOB 14:1–2; 1 JOHN 2:17—Ps. 102:26–27—HEB. 13:8.

Be filled with the Holy Spirit. Tell of your joy to each other by singing the Songs of David and church songs. Sing in your heart to the Lord—Let the teaching of Christ and His words keep on living in you. These make your lives rich and full of wisdom. Keep on teaching and helping each other. Sing the Songs of David and the church songs and the songs of heaven with hearts full of thanks to God.

My mouth will speak the praise of the Lord. And all flesh will honor His holy name forever and ever.

Praise the Lord! For it is good to sing praises to our God. For it is pleasing and praise is right. Sing to the Lord with thanks. Sing praises to our God on the harp.

I heard a voice coming from heaven. It was like the sound of rushing water and of loud thunder. The voice I heard was like people playing music on their harps.

1 COR. 14:15; EPH. 5:18–19—COL. 3:16; PS. 145:21; PS. 147:1, 7; REV. 14:2.

You know you were not bought and made free from sin by paying gold or silver which comes to an end. . .not saved from the punishment of sin by the way of life that you were given from your early fathers. . . . The blood of Christ saved you. . .blood. . .of great worth. Christ was given as a lamb without sin and without spot—He carried our sins in His own body when He died on a cross.

He gave this loving-favor to us through His much-loved Son.

As living stones in the building God is making also . . .His religious leaders giving yourselves to God through Jesus Christ—Christian brothers, I ask you from my heart to give your bodies to God because of His loving-kindness to us. Let your bodies be a living and holy gift given to God. . . . This is the true worship that you should give Him.

One Who can keep you from falling and can bring you before Himself free from all sin. He can give you great joy as you stand before Him in His shining-greatness. He is the only God. . . . May He have shining-greatness and honor and power and the right to do all things. . .He has it now, and He will have this forever.

Lev. 1:4; 1 Pet. 1:18–19—1 Pet. 2:24; Eph. 1:6; 1 Pet. 2:5—Rom. 12:1—Jude 24–25.

The woman saw that the tree was good for food [the desires of our flesh], and pleasing to the eyes [the things our eyes see and want], and could fill the desire of making one wise [the pride of this life]. So she took of its fruit and ate. She also gave some to her husband, and he ate.

The devil came tempting [Jesus] and said, If You are the Son of God, tell these stones to be made into bread [desires of our flesh]. But Jesus said. . .Man is not to live on bread only. Man is to live by every word that God speaks. The devil. . .had Jesus look at all the nations of the world to see how great they were [the things our eyes see and want, the pride of this life]. . . . Jesus said to the devil, Get away, Satan.

Because Jesus was tempted as we are and suffered as we do, He understands us and He is able to help us when we are tempted.

The man who does not give up when tests come is happy.

HEB. 4:15; GEN. 3:6; [1 JOHN 2:16]; MATT. 4:3–4, 8–10; [1 JOHN 2:16]—HEB. 2:18; JAMES 1:12.

Be kind to me, O Lord, for I am weak. O Lord, heal me for my bones are shaken. My soul is in great suffering. But You, O Lord, how long? Return, O Lord. Set my soul free. Save me because of Your loving-kindness—My heart is in pain within me. The fears of death have come upon me. I have begun shaking with fear. Fear has power over me. And I say, If only I had wings like a dove, I would fly away and be at rest.

You must be willing to wait without giving up.

They were still looking up to heaven, watching Him go. All at once two men dressed in white stood beside them. They said, You men of the country of Galilee, why do you stand looking up into heaven? This same Jesus Who was taken from you into heaven will return in the same way you saw Him go up into heaven—But we are citizens of heaven. Christ, the One Who saves from the punishment of sin, will be coming down from heaven again—The great hope and the coming of our great God and the One Who saves, Christ Jesus.

Isa. 38:14; Ps. 6:2–4—Ps. 55:4–6; Heb. 10:36; Acts 1:10–11—Phil. 3:20—Titus 2:13.

I am the Good Shepherd. I know My sheep—But the truth of God cannot be changed. It says, The Lord knows those who are His. And, Everyone who says he is a Christian must turn away from sin!

The Lord is good, a safe place in times of trouble. And He knows those who come to Him to be safe—Do not hurt the earth or the sea or the trees until we have put the mark of God on the foreheads of the servants He owns.

You put your trust in Christ. Then God marked you by giving you His Holy Spirit as a promise. . .that we will receive everything God has for us—God is the One Who makes our faith and your faith strong in Christ. He has set us apart for Himself.

I will write on him the name of My God and the name of the city of My God. It is the new Jerusalem. . .will come down from My God out of heaven. I will write My new name on him—This is the name it will be called: The Lord makes us right and good.

REV. 22:4; JOHN 10:14—2 TIM. 2:19; NAH. 1:7—REV. 7:3; EPH. 1:13–14—2 COR. 1:21; REV. 3:12—JER. 33:16.

God has raised up His Son Jesus and has sent Him to you first to give God's favor to each of you who will turn away from his sinful ways.

Let us thank the God and Father of our Lord Jesus Christ. It was through His loving-kindness that we were born again to a new life and have a hope that never dies. . .because Jesus was raised from the dead—Saved by His life.

The One Who saves, Christ Jesus. . .gave Himself for us. . .buying us with His blood and making us free from all sin. . .so His people could be clean and want to do good—Be holy in every part of your life. Be like the Holy One Who chose you.

The God and Father of our Lord Jesus Christ. . .has already given us a taste of what heaven is like—Christ is not only God-like, He is God in human flesh. When you have Christ, you are complete—From Him Who has so much we have all received loving-favor, one loving-favor after another.

God did not keep His own Son for Himself but gave Him for us all. Then with His Son, will He not give us all things?

ACTS 3:26; 1 PET. 1:3—ROM. 5:10; TITUS 2:13–14—1 PET. 1:15; EPH. 1:3—COL. 2:9–10—JOHN 1:16; ROM. 8:32.

Remember Your Word to Your servant, for You have given me hope—O Lord, I am having a hard time. Keep me safe.

Heaven and earth will pass away, but My Words will not pass away—Know in all your hearts and in all your souls that not one of all the good promises the Lord your God made to you has been broken. All have come true for you. Not one of them has been broken.

Do not be afraid. May peace be with you. Be strong and have strength of heart. And when he had spoken to me, I received strength, and said, May my lord speak, for you have given me strength—Be strong. . . . Do the work, for I am with you, says the Lord of All.—Not by strength nor by power, but by My Spirit, says the Lord of All.

Be strong with the Lord's strength.

Ps. 119:28; Ps. 119:49—Isa. 38:14; Luke 21:33—Josh. 23:14; Dan. 10:19—Hag. 2:4—Zech. 4:6; Eph. 6:10.

This is what we heard Him tell us. We are passing it on to you. God is light. There is no darkness in Him—God ...said, The light will shine in darkness.... He is the One Who made His light shine in our hearts. This brings us the light of knowing God's shining-greatness which is seen in Christ's face—The Word was God. Life began by Him. His Life was the Light for men—If we live in the light as He is in the light, we share what we have in God with each other. And the blood of Jesus Christ, His Son, makes our lives clean from all sin.

Your Word have I hid in my heart, that I may not sin against You—You are made clean by the words I have spoken to you.

At one time you lived in darkness. Now you are living in the light that comes from the Lord. Live as children who have the light of the Lord—But you are a chosen group of people. You are the King's religious leaders. You are a holy nation. You belong to God. He has done this for you so you can tell others how God has called you out of darkness into His great light.

Ps. 119:130; 1 John 1:5—2 Cor. 4:6—John 1:1, 4—1 John 1:7; Ps 119:11—John 15:3; Eph. 5:8—1 Pet. 2:9.

The man right with God will live by faith—Then Noah built an altar to the Lord. He took of every clean animal and every clean bird, and gave burnt gifts in worship on the altar. Then the Lord smelled a pleasing smell—From the beginning of the world...Lamb Who was killed.

Now that we have been made right with God by putting our trust in Him, we have peace with Him. It is because of what our Lord Jesus Christ did for us.

No person will be made right with God by doing what the Law says. The Law shows us how sinful we are. But now God has made another way to make men right with Himself. It is not by the Law. The Law and the early preachers tell about it. Men become right with God by putting their trust in Jesus Christ. God will accept men if they come this way. All men are the same to God.

We give thanks to God through our Lord Jesus Christ. Through Him we have been brought back to God.

Who can say anything against the people God has chosen? It is God Who says they are right with Himself. He called to Himself also those He chose. Those He called, He made right with Himself.

GEN. 6:9; GAL. 3:11—GEN. 8:20–21—REV. 13:8; ROM. 5:1; ROM. 3:20–22; ROM. 5:11; ROM. 8:33, 30.

The end of the world is near. You must be the boss over your mind. Keep awake so you can pray—Keep awake! Watch at all times. The devil is working against you . . .walking around like a hungry lion with his mouth open. He is looking for someone to eat—Only be careful. Keep watch over your life. Or you might forget the things you have seen. Do not let them leave your heart for the rest of your life—For the one right with God lives by faith. If anyone turns back, I will not be pleased with him . . .We are not of those people who turn back and are lost. Instead, we have faith to be saved from the punishment of sin.

What I say to you, I say to all. Watch!

Do not fear, for I am with you. Do not be afraid, for I am your God. I will give you strength, and for sure I will help you. Yes, I will hold you up with My right hand that is right and good. For I am the Lord your God Who holds your right hand.

REV. 3:2; 1 PET. 4:7; 1 PET. 5:8—DEUT. 4:9—HEB. 10:38–39: MARK 13:37; ISA. 41:10, 13.

His loving-kindness lasts forever—The Lord is slow to anger and filled with loving-kindness—Who is a God like You, Who forgives sin and the wrong-doing of Your chosen people who are left? He does not stay angry forever because He is happy to show loving kindness. He will again have loving-pity on us. He will crush our sins under foot. Yes, You will throw all our sins into the deep sea—It was not because we worked to be right with God. It was because of His loving-kindness that He washed our sins away.

We give thanks to the God and Father of our Lord Jesus Christ. He is our Father Who shows us loving-kindness and our God Who gives us comfort. He gives us comfort in all our troubles. Then we can comfort other people who have the same troubles. We give the same kind of comfort God gives us.

[Jesus] had to be one of us to be our Religious Leader to go between God and us. He had loving-pity on us and He was faithful. He gave Himself as a gift to die on a cross for our sins so that God would not hold these sins against us any longer. Because Jesus was tempted as we are and suffered as we do, He understands us and He is able to help us when we are tempted.

Ps. 77:8; Ps. 136:23—Num. 14:18—Mic. 7:18–19— Titus 3:5; 2 Cor. 1:3–4; Heb. 2:17–18.

Lot looked and saw that the Jordan valley was well watered everywhere like the garden of the Lord... (before the Lord destroyed Sodom and Gomorrah.) So Lot chose all the Jordan valley for himself.

Lot...his own soul which was right with God was troubled because of their sinful ways.

Do not be fooled. You cannot fool God. A man will get back whatever he plants!—Remember Lot's wife!

Do not be joined together with those who do not belong to Christ. How can that which is good get along with that which is bad? How can light be in the same place with darkness? The Lord has said, So come out from among them. Do not be joined to them. Touch nothing that is sinful. And I will receive you—Have nothing to do with them. At one time you lived in darkness. Now you are living in the light that comes from the Lord. Live as children who have the light of the Lord in them. Learn how to please the Lord. Have nothing to do with the bad things done in darkness. Instead, show that these things are wrong.

GEN. 13:10–11; 2 PET. 2:7–8; GAL. 6:7—LUKE 17:32; 2 COR. 6:14, 17—EPH. 5:7–8, 10–11.

If the Lord will be with me,
I will drive them out just as the Lord said.

God has said, I will never leave you or let you be alone .... So we can say for sure, The Lord is my Helper. I am not afraid of anything man can do to me—I will come in the strength of the Lord God. I will tell about how right and good You are, and You alone.

The work of being right and good will give peace. From the right and good work will come quiet trust forever.

Stand up.... Wear a belt of truth around your body. Wear a piece of iron over your chest which is being right with God. Our fight is not with people. It is against the leaders and the powers and the spirits of darkness in this world. It is against the demon world that works in the heavens. Because of this, put on all the things God gives you to fight with. Then you will be able to stand in that sinful day. When it is all over, you will still be standing.

The Lord is with you. . . . Go in this strength of yours.

Josh. 14:12; Heb. 13:5–6—Ps. 71:16; Isa. 32:17; Eph. 6:14, 12–13—Jud. 6:12, 14.

Yet You are holy. The praises Israel gives You are Your throne—Do not come near. Take your shoes off your feet. For the place where you are standing is holy ground ...I am the God of your father, the God of Abraham, the God of Isaac, and the God of Jacob. Then Moses hid his face. For he was afraid to look at God—To whom will you compare Me, that I should be like him? says the Holy One—I am the Lord your God, the Holy One of Israel, Who saves you.... I, even I, am the Lord. There is no one who saves except Me.

Be holy in every part of your life. Be like the Holy One Who chose you. The Holy Writings say, You must be holy, for I am holy—Do you not know that your body is a house of God where the Holy Spirit lives? .... Now you belong to God. You do not belong to yourselves— We are the house of the living God. God has said, I will live in them and will walk among them. I will be their God and they will be My people—Do two men walk together unless they have made an agreement?

Rev. 4:8; Ps. 22:3—Exod. 3:5–6—Isa. 40:25—Isa. 43:3, 11; 1 Pet. 1:15–16—1 Cor. 6:19—2 Cor. 6:16— Amos 3:3.

See! I stand at the door and knock. If anyone hears My voice and opens the door, I will come in to him and we will eat together—Tell me, O you whom my soul loves. In what field do you feed your flock? Where do your sheep lie down at noon? Why should I need to look for you beside the flocks of your friends?—I found him whom my soul loves. I held on to him and would not let him go.

May my loved one come into his garden and eat its best fruits.—I have come into my garden—I did not say to the children of Jacob, Look for Me for nothing.

I am with you always, even to the end of the world—I will never leave you or let you be alone—For where two or three are gathered together in My name, there I am with them—The world will see Me no more. You will see Me.

LUKE 24:29; REV. 3:20—SONG OF SOL. 1:7—SONG OF SOL. 3:4; SONG OF SOL. 4:16—SONG OF SOL. 5:1—ISA. 45:19; MATT. 28:20—HEB. 13:5—MATT. 18:20—JOHN 14:19.

Abraham did not doubt God's promise. His faith in God was strong, and he gave thanks to God. He was sure God was able to do what He had promised. Abraham put his trust in God and was made right with Him. The words, He was made right with God, were not for Abraham only. They were for us also. God will make us right with Himself the same way He did Abraham, if we put our trust in God Who raised Jesus our Lord from the dead.

God promised to give the world to him and to all his family after him. . . . He promised to give the world to Abraham because he put his trust in God. This made him right with God.

A man right with God lives by faith—Let us hold on to the hope we say we have and not be changed. We can trust God that He will do what He promised—But our God is in the heavens. He does whatever He wants to do.—God can do all things. You are happy because you believed. Everything will happen as the Lord told you it would happen.

GEN. 15:6; ROM. 4:20–24; ROM. 4:13; ROM. 1:17—HEB. 10:23—PS. 115:3—LUKE 1:37, 45.

My holy nation does not belong to this world. If My holy nation were of this world, My helpers would fight. . . . My holy nation is not of this world—He is waiting there for God to make of those who have hated Him a place to rest His feet.

The nations of the world have become the holy nation of our Lord and of His Christ. He will be the Leader forever—You have made them to be a holy nation of religious leaders to work for our God. They will be the leaders on the earth—I saw thrones. Those who were sitting there were given the power to judge. . . . They lived again and were leaders along with Christ for 1,000 years— Then the ones right with God will shine as the sun in the holy nation of their Father—Do not be afraid, little flock. Your Father wants to give you the holy nation of God.

As My Father has given Me a holy nation, I will give you the right to eat and drink at My table in My holy nation. You will sit on thrones and judge the twelve family groups of the Jewish nation.

May Your holy nation come.

1 Thess. 2:12; John 18:36—Heb. 10:13; Rev. 11:15— Rev. 5:10—Rev. 20:4—Matt. 13:43—Luke 12:32; Luke 22:29–30; Matt. 6:10.

So we can say for sure, The Lord is my Helper. I am not afraid of anything man can do to me.

See, I am with you. I will care for you everywhere you go. And I will bring you again to this land. For I will not leave you until I have done all the things I promised you—Be strong and have strength of heart. Do not be afraid or shake with fear because of them. For the Lord your God is the One Who goes with you. He will be faithful to you. He will not leave you alone.

Demas left me. He loved the things of this world. At my first trial no one helped me. Everyone left me. I hope this will not be held against them. But the Lord was with me. He gave me power—For my father and my mother have left me. But the Lord will take care of me.

I am with you always, even to the end of the world—I am the Living One. I was dead, but look, I am alive forever—I will not leave you without help as children without parents. I will come to you—Peace I leave with you.

HEB. 13:5; HEB. 13:6; GEN. 28:15—DEUT. 31:6; 2 TIM. 4:10, 16–17—PS. 27:10; MATT. 28:20—REV. 1:18—JOHN 14:18—JOHN 14:27.

*Teacher, we have worked all night and
we have caught nothing. But because
You told me to, I will let the net down.*

All power has been given to Me in heaven and on earth.
Go and make followers of all the nations. Baptize them
in the name of the Father and of the Son and of the Holy
Spirit. . . . And I am with you always, even to the end of
the world.

The holy nation of heaven is like a big net which
was let down into the sea.

I cannot be proud because I preach the Good News.
I have been told to do it. It would be bad for me if I do
not preach the Good News. . . . I have become like every
person so in every way I might lead some to Christ.

Do not let yourselves get tired of doing good. If we
do not give up, we will get what is coming to us at the
right time.—My Word. . .will not return to Me empty.
It will do what I want it to do, and will carry out My
plan well.—The one who plants or the one who waters
is not the important one. God is the important One. He
makes it grow.

LUKE 5:5; MATT. 28:18–20; MATT. 13:47; 1 COR. 9:16,
22; GAL 6:9—ISA. 55:11—1 COR 3:7.

> *For the holy nation of heaven is like a man who was going to a country far away. He called together the servants he owned and gave them his money to use. . . as he was able to use it.*

Do you not know that when you give yourself as a servant to be owned by someone, that one becomes your owner?

The Holy Spirit works in each person in one way or another for the good of all—God has given each of you a gift. Use it to help each other. This will show God's loving-favor—A servant must be faithful to his owner. This is expected of him—The man who receives much will have to give much. If much is given to a man to take care of, men will expect to get more from him.

Who is able for such a work?—I can do all things because Christ gives me the strength.

MATT. 25:14–15; ROM. 6:16; 1 COR. 12:7—1 PET. 4:10—
1 COR. 4:2—LUKE 12:48; 2 COR. 2:16—PHIL. 4:13.

Then David said, Is there anyone left of the family of Saul, to whom I may show kindness because of Jonathan?

Come, you who have been called by My Father. Come into the holy nation that has been made ready for you before the world was made. For I was hungry and you gave Me food to eat. I was thirsty and you gave Me water to drink. I was a stranger and you gave Me a room. I had no clothes and you gave Me clothes to wear. I was sick and you cared for Me. I was in prison and you came to see Me. Then the King will say, For sure, I tell you, because you did it to one of the least of My brothers, you have done it to Me—Anyone who gives a cup of cold water to one of these little ones because he follows Me, will not lose his reward.

Remember to do good and help each other. Gifts like this please God—God always does what is right. He will not forget the work you did to help the Christians and the work you are still doing to help them. This shows your love for Christ.

Rom. 12:13; 2 Sam. 9:1; Matt. 25: 34–36, 40—Matt. 10:42; Heb. 13:16—Heb. 6:10.

After a long time the owner of those servants came back. He wanted to know what had been done with his money. The one who had received the five pieces of money worth much came and handed him five pieces more. He said, Sir, you gave me five pieces of money. See! I used it and made five more pieces. His owner said to him, You have done well. You are a good and faithful servant. You have been faithful over a few things. I will put many things in your care. Come and share my joy.

For all of us must stand before Christ when He says who is guilty or not guilty. Each one will receive pay for what he has done. He will be paid for the good or the bad done while he lived in this body.

I have fought a good fight. I have finished the work I was to do. I have kept the faith. There is a crown which comes from being right with God. The Lord, the One Who will judge, will give it to me on that great day when He comes again. I will not be the only one to receive a crown. All those who love to think of His coming and are looking for Him will receive one also.

I am coming very soon. Hold on to what you have so no one can take your crown.

PROV. 11:18; MATT. 25:19–21; 2 COR. 5:10; 2 TIM. 4:7–8; REV. 3:11.

God is not a man, that He should lie. He is not a son of man, that He should be sorry for what He has said. Has He said, and will He not do it? Has He spoken, and will He not keep His Word?

God made a promise. He wanted to show Abraham that He would never change His mind. So He made the promise in His own name. God gave these two things that cannot be changed and God cannot lie. We who have turned to Him can have great comfort knowing that He will do what He has promised—So if God wants you to suffer, give yourself to Him. He will do what is right for you. He made you and He is faithful.

I know the One in Whom I have put my trust. I am sure He is able to keep safe that which I have trusted to Him until the day He comes again—The One Who called you is faithful and will do what He promised—Jesus says yes to all of God's many promises. It is through Jesus that we say, Let it be so, when we give thanks to God.

1 Cor. 10:13; Num. 23:19; Heb. 6:17–18—1 Pet. 4:19; 2 Tim. 1:12—1 Thess. 5:24—2 Cor. 1:20.

The Lord is my light and the One Who saves me. Whom should I fear? The Lord is the strength of my life. Of whom should I be afraid?—He gives strength to the weak. And He gives power to him who has little strength. Even very young men get tired and become weak and strong young men trip and fall. But they who wait upon the Lord will get new strength. They will rise up with wings like eagles. They will run and not get tired. They will walk and not become weak—My body and my heart may grow weak, but God is the strength of my heart and all I need forever.

Since God is for us, who can be against us?—The Lord is with me. I will not be afraid of what man can do to me—Through You we will push away those who hate us. Through Your name we will walk over those who rise up against us—But we have power over all these things through Jesus Who loves us so much.

So get ready and work, and may the Lord be with you.

JOSH. 1:18; PS. 27:1—ISA. 40:29–31—PS. 73:26; ROM. 8:31—PS. 118:6—PS. 44:5—ROM. 8:37; 1 CHRON. 22:16.

SCRIPTURE INDEX

Old Testament

New Testament